Digital Media and Documentary

Adrian Miles
Editor

Digital Media and Documentary

Antipodean Approaches

palgrave
macmillan

Editor
Adrian Miles
RMIT University
Melbourne, VIC, Australia

ISBN 978-3-319-68642-4 ISBN 978-3-319-68643-1 (eBook)
https://doi.org/10.1007/978-3-319-68643-1

Library of Congress Control Number: 2017956104

Printed on acid-free paper

This Palgrave Pivot imprint is published by Springer Nature
The registered company is Springer International Publishing AG
The registered company address is: Gewerbestrasse 11, 6330 Cham, Switzerland

Dedicated to Charlie, Jasper, and Cleo.

Contents

Thirteen Points of View from Afar 1
Adrian Miles

Moments of Noticing: 'I See You' as a Speculative Work Towards an Essayistic List Practice for Interactive Documentary 13
Hannah Brasier

Documentary, Instructions, and Experiences of Place 29
Bettina Frankham

The Documentary Designer: A List of Propositions for Interactive Documentary Practice Online 49
Seth Keen

Ambient Media Making, Auto-Documentary, and Affect 69
Adrian Miles

Miniature and Series: The Re-invention of the Epistolary Form in the Work of Alexander Hahn 83
Cathie Payne

***24Frames 24Hours*: An Emerging Form of Workshop-Generated Documentary** 101
Max Schleser

Index 111

Notes on Contributors

Hannah Brasier is in the final stages of completing a project-led PhD at RMIT University in Melbourne, Australia. Her research considers how the list provides a method of ***documentary attending*** that enables a multilinear video practice. She has created a series of multilinear video works using Korsakow, and her research interests are the essay film, interactive documentary, experimental cinema, posthumanism, and new materialism. Hannah has presented at national and international conferences and is a founding member of non/fictionLab's Docuverse symposium.

Bettina Frankham is a practice-led researcher in digital media and teaches in the Faculty of Arts and Social Sciences at the University of Technology Sydney. She has a background of industry experience that spans multiple forms of media including television, radio, and web production. Her research interests include art and documentary intersections, expanded documentary practice, and the impact of digital culture on creative media production. She is currently investigating the shift towards documentary as a rhetorical experience and is exploring the role of the digital in understandings of what documentary can do.

Seth Keen teaches new media at RMIT University in Melbourne, Australia. Seth is an audiovisual media designer and producer who collaborates on transdisciplinary projects that focus on solutions to real-world problems. He provides expertise that integrates his past industry experience as a television documentary producer with new media research. Interested in digital media innovation, he collaborates with research, cultural, and commercial partners on the design of audiovisual production frameworks and digital platforms.

Adrian Miles is co-director of the non/fictionLab, and Deputy Dean Learning and Teaching at RMIT University in Melbourne, Australia. Adrian does research on networked video, interactive documentary, and computational nonfiction, from a materialist point of view with a Deleuzean cinematic inflection. Adrian's research interests also include pedagogies for new media, digital video poetics, and experimental academic writing practices.

Cathie Payne researches cinema and media arts as "modes of thought," and what they bring to light about current ways of seeing nature, space, and time. She is a writer and new media producer and worked with the Australian Museum, Australian Film, Television and Radio School (AFTRS), Museum of Applied Arts and Sciences, and ABC Science on works about cultural heritage and climate science. She is currently working on a documentary, and a series of video and audio works. She teaches at the University of Newcastle in Australia, and lives in Sydney.

Max Schleser is a filmmaker who explores smartphones and mobile media for creative transformation and media production. His experimental and collaborative documentaries are screened at film festivals, galleries and museums internationally (www.schleser.nz). He is the creative director of the storytelling platform *24Frames 24Hours* (www.24frames24hours.org.nz) and creative co-producer of Viewfinders (www.viewfinders.gallery). He co-founded MINA, the Mobile Innovation Network Australasia (www.mina.pro), and curates the annual International Mobile Innovation Screening. Max is a senior lecturer in Film and TV at Swinburne University of Technology, Melbourne, Australia.

Thirteen Points of View from Afar

Adrian Miles

Abstract This chapter discusses the milieu of academic anthologies and the particular concerns that they arise from, and to. It argues that this anthology provides a variety of reports from scholar practitioners that offer a series of views for what interactive documentary practice is, and might be. It argues that for these practitioner scholars the network emerges as a site of practice, and that as a place for making requires different affordances and understandings than that of legacy documentary. It concludes with a series of propositions about the World Wide Web as a socio-technical system that encourages granular, distributed, and relational forms.

Keywords Interactive documentary • Multilinear narrative

One

This anthology collects and celebrates recent work by a cohort of scholar practitioners that have, through conversations, conferences, and collaborations, developed a shared and common argot of practice and theory. This argot provides the writing collected here with a scale that is an effect (even today) of the particular geographical distance and remove that

A. Miles (✉)
School of Media and Communication, RMIT University,
Melbourne, VIC, Australia

A. Miles (ed.), *Digital Media and Documentary*,
https://doi.org/10.1007/978-3-319-68643-1_1

Australasia has from what are the centres and mediators of disciplinary authority and commerce. This is then a distinctly antipodean collection, with the work minor, in Deleuze and Guattari's sense of how "a minority constructs within a major" (p. 16). By virtue of this burrowing, it can, as Deleuze and Guattari memorably characterise, make the major stammer and stutter. The writing that follows sketches the margins and edges of new practices that are described and advocated for. It is a local writing, specific to individual histories, institutions, disciplines, and students, and relies on the tools and resources each of us have, ready to hand. This is a post-occupation appropriation and making do, cobbling together new practices and habits from amongst the known and the deeply unfamiliar. These chapters then have the quality of being loose accounts in their describing and analysis and are propositions for what can be.

Two

The gestation of this anthology was an entanglement amongst a conference, theory that informs practice, practice that seeks to be understood theoretically, provisional constellations of equipment, protocols, and actions, and geography. The intent of this anthology, while collecting recent Australasian work about interactive documentary, digital nonfiction, and media making more broadly, was to experiment with forms of scholarly writing. This experimentation hoped to use writing practices that could accommodate and acknowledge entangled voices and forms while also doing the evidenced-based, contestable argument of scholarly writing. A subjective wondering that allowed for the agency of thought, phrase, voice, and work that was situated (Haraway) or even a thick writing (Geertz). A writing, so to speak, that was as contextually dense, self-aware, and mediated as the practices described and discussed.

This has not, by and large, happened and this is an intriguing problem and outcome in its own right. That this has happened is in no way a cause for any particular concern as the writing that follows is that of practitioner scholars well versed and acculturated to the academic vernaculars of our respective institutions. The conservativeness of this might surprise, as the writers here generally insist on the autonomy and authority of practice and the artefacts that are its consequence, but generally have not applied this to their own writing. Some do stray from the formulaic structures of academic writing and argument, whether through speculation (Frankham), personal commentary (Brasier), or the use of declarative imperatives

(Keen). However, it is also fair to say that where each of the practitioners makes work that has some element or quality of the experimental the writing, for the most part, does not follow suit. It is, as it turns out, not as comfortable as imagined to be an academic essayist.

Three

An academic book, I like to think, is a response to a problem. This problem might be a question, something like a curiosity or perhaps even a humble wondering. The problem may be an obvious and large concern, something we all agree matters. Or the problem may not be so apparent and the work of the writing then becomes one of persuading us of its importance. In either case the problems that initiate academic books can be approached with the vantage of a sweeping view, surveying a panorama of peaks. Or they may choose to place themselves deep in a valley, sitting by the creek paying particular, close attention to the minutiae of the near to hand.

I write this in an office inside a middle-ranking department inside a middle-ranking university. I write this within a modern city that in its multicultural internationalism is a pleasantly provincial place. This is an Australasian view upon questions that arise from making interactive documentary.

Four

The problem that an academic book responds to and the situatedness of its writing are entangled throughout this anthology. The contributors found themselves, as much by happenstance, bought together by their participation at a conference in regional New South Wales in 2014. Each author has an interest in how media making intersects with scholarship, and has ambitions of thinking with and through its media. As a consequence, the research performed here proceeds from the individual forms and works that have emerged from particular nonfiction audiovisual and networked media practices. To the extent that each writer grounds their study in the affordances and practical activity of realised or speculative projects the theoretical writing develops a pragmatic, near to hand, quality. In this way this is a writing of the valley, and such valley writing is one response to the problem of how to write, academically, to one's own experimental digital documentary practice.

Five

This anthology responds to indistinct precursors. These precursors are indistinct because none, by themselves, are clear enough that they neatly draw a line through its chapters. They are indistinct because a conversation between scholarly research, creative practice, documentary, and networked time-based media is what we hope emerges as the use and value of this book. These indistinct precursors include a screen practice research conference, panels and debates at this conference, a proposal that these panels and debates could form a book, the loose minor theoretical vernacular we have developed amongst ourselves from our shared situations and practices, a common experience of wrestling with efforts to legitimate and reify media making into the major language of capital "R" research and, finally, an increasing rigour in how to conceive of interactive documentary projects as research instruments of creative nonfiction.

Six

Andrew Murphie has elegantly described how technical media has exploded its forms, varieties, and methods of doing. A significant quality of this explosion is a dramatic change in the scale and temporality of media, and media making. When access was scarce because of cost, technical complexity, and the constraints upon broadcast, exhibition, and distribution, it took time and significant resources to record, compile, and then distribute technical media. As a consequence, we wanted the things made to matter, to be significant, even to some extent to be monuments. Now, with innumerable technical media apps and services available on our smart phones, and a planetary scale distribution system immediately near to hand, technical media, like writing, can extend from monuments to minor asides. As Murphie argues:

> As technics diversifies this leads to more 'ends'. These technical ends become our main concern, our focus. Yet these ends are no longer as grand—no longer transcendent. They are smaller ends—more immediate and more immanent. Indeed they are often no longer ends at all, instead becoming means without ends. (188)

This provides another heuristic by which to understand the chapters curated here. This diversification of technics clarifies the distance and differences between legacy nonfiction forms and practices and those emerging in the wake of this explosion of technical means and ends. This distance and difference is evident in the loss of authority that legacy media is experiencing as they can no longer rely on or assume a legitimacy that relies upon confusing professional privilege and technological scarcity as a given. In the case of documentary particular constellations of technology and their attending practices have been understood to engage with, and make arguments about, the world, yet the structure and form of how these arguments were made was constrained because the only shapes available through technical media were resolutely linear, time bound, and sequential. Unsurprisingly then, narrative, beautiful in a myriad of ways, became a governing principle. In this way narrative became part of the technics of documentary and was relied upon as a cornerstone of nonfiction audiovisual practice to confer coherence.

What happens, though, when technics proliferate? When filming, recording, storing, manipulating, and distributing media is near to hand and immediate? Here the imperative for legacy media to cohere dissolves. Media is now transitory and ephemeral (Grainge), small, intimate, and personal (van Dijck). It increasingly becomes a flow of signals and relays rather than monuments chiselled into canons, archives, and our other aspirations of significance and permanence.

These ephemeral and minor qualities are evident in the diversity of voice, tone, argument, and ideas that the following chapters explore. Novel propositions emerge about listing, noticing, sketching, scale, and relationality. The value of these propositions, for me and you, will vary.

Seven

This is an anthology that does not offer an account of interactive documentary in general. It can be read and used as offering a series of facets, or points of view, from which to think about the current practices and protocols that need to be loosely collected together when considering interactive documentary.

This anthology then is a response to Jon Dovey's argument for a "post–industrial understanding of knowledge exchange processes" (p. 255). Such processes "would seek to understand the complex linkages between different part of the creative system as a whole" (p. 255). This is realised in how different links can be found between the chapters with their respective ideas and claims. This linking becomes an invitation to recognise the commonalities and distinctions between the authors to productively recognise and build upon these differences.

Eight

Any description of Dovey's "knowledge exchange processes" has to acknowledge the network and the use of the World Wide Web. In relation to interactive documentary, this includes the use of the web to research documentary content, seek answers about technical issues with hardware and software, exchanging emails to assist collaboration, interviews, travel, bookings, site information, legals, financial transactions, and so on. There is the use of social media to promote and document creative and scholarly work. This list would include the use of online networks to distribute media files during production for editing, promotion, collaboration, archiving and backup, and the distribution of a final release. Increasingly, these networks will be used by the equipment and artefacts themselves, what we know as the "Internet of Things" (IoT) as our cameras, sound recorders, and other field documentation devices and equipment utilise different communicative protocols to exchange information amongst themselves, and to other places. Increasingly, as we adapt to these new socio-technical assemblages, these new socio-technical assemblages will adapt us.

Or, as Dovey in the same essay notes "[t]o understand network media close up we do need to adapt our professional practice and our research projects to the networked online environment" (p. 251). This is an invitation that is now common as networked online environments are ubiquitous for all our media making and scholarship. The rub lies in what it what means for documentary to "adapt" to this environment for making and also the conduct and form of scholarship. Descriptions of activities is one avenue by which to conduct such scholarship and it is in this describing that the possible links and connections between parts is realised. This is because description invites attention and analysis that is complex and sophisticated without recourse to discourses that seek to account for and enclose argument within an envelope of epistemological exhaustion.

Dovey's point describes the difference between using the network as a more or less mute vehicle, "dumb" infrastructure, versus recognising the affordances of networked online environments and the agency that such affordances require and enable. What these networks *do* matters, and being able to identify, describe, and understand what they do requires participation in them, a going native as it were. This is harder to achieve than it appears because many of us bring the paradigms established during a time of industrial media and scholarship to the network, and so we misread the affordances and agency of this network as we continue to try to use it for what we have always done.

Hence, it is through recognising the affordances of digital, networked, media, what it can do, that we will make working in this domain different to what we have learnt from non-digital, not networked media. These affordances arise from miniaturisation, portability, a near zero cost of recording, infinite reproducibility, and the pliability for storage, exchange, and random, nonlinear access that turning media into binary code and signals allows.

These underwrite the well-documented changes afforded by the World Wide Web with its ease and scale of distribution, collaboration, and viral sharing through the exchange of tokens of endorsement via comments, likes, dislikes, favouriting, and embedding. All of these rely on social and technical protocols that have become the norm for social media platforms. Less obviously is that these affordances, in themselves, don't much affect, or have implications for, the practice or forms of nonfiction media making because they can be as happily applied to a feature-length film as to a clip on YouTube. It is then those other affordances, those that have been less readily noticed, understood, and adopted by interactive documentary, that will come to matter, and which all the authors here address. Such a list of affordances includes granularity, addressability, porosity, and relationality, as well as the more specific procedural and generative attributes of the computer as a calculating machine.

Nine

As a socio-technical network the World Wide Web was designed to be adept at bringing small, relatively self-contained things together into collated or curated new wholes. Instagram, by way of example, consists of individual photographs and videos that are loosely and informally curated into collections based on who any individual chooses to "follow," as well as being aggregated automatically by geolocation and hashtags. Any individual photograph on Instagram can be endorsed through "liking" or by the use of system-generated HTML that allows others to embed these photograph into discrete, different, and dispersed web pages. These are the "small bits, loosely joined," as popular commentator David Weinberger memorably noted. This mixing of scale, of small parts that are easily joined into larger wholes, is possible because these small media artefacts are granular, addressable, and porous.

Granularity is understood as how larger whole things can be made up of smaller parts where, and this is fundamental, these smaller parts are also whole things. Addressability refers to the way these smaller parts as well as the larger collections they form have their own network address, allowing all to be recognised and used as separate and discrete media objects. The manner in which these smaller parts, and the new and variable larger wholes they combine to become, can be shared and distributed makes everything porous. This porousness describes the softness and fluidity of the edges of the things in these networks. These soft edges, in the example of Instagram, are how an image or a collection of images easily finds itself popping up embedded in a blog or perhaps Facebook from where it is then liked and now appears in potentially millions of feeds. Fluidity is apparent in the continually shifting contexts that now surround these photos as media artefacts by virtue of their porousness.

An outcome of being granular, addressable, and porous is a complicated relationality. This relationality, which cinema is intimately familiar with through Kuleshov's famous experiments, is what editing is and does. However, such relationality is dramatically and qualitatively different for audiovisual media in networked contexts. This qualitative change occurs in the different types of relations now established between media parts. Unlike our experience of legacy film and video where the relations between pieces of media are static and stable, within interactive systems they have the capacity to always vary. This enables works that are ephemeral, that change between individual readings. What I read and view in an individual work could very well be quite different to what someone else views, not because the media components used are different (though they could be), but because the order and sequences in which they appear are dynamic. And, as editing in cinema helps us understand, it is not only the content of the shot, but the order and relations in which shots and sequences are arranged, that matters.

Finally, in this suite of network affordances the two qualities of the procedural and generative must be included. The procedural describes rule-governed actions and behaviours. Computers are highly adept at performing such rule-defined actions (it is their default condition) so they are excellent machines for undertaking procedural work. The generative is understood as the iteration of a simple procedure or set of rules in a way that allows for complex systems, structures, and therefore patterns, to emerge. There are many examples of generative structures and systems in the world—the weather perhaps being the most obvious and common—and in the context of computers it is procedural iteration that allows generative patterns and relations to emerge where often these patterns are unknown and unknowable in advance.

These different attributes are implicit to the contributions that follow. What becomes explicit, and occurs as a series of immanent threads, is the importance and recurrence of these attributes as listing, noticing, sketching, scale, and, eventually, relationality.

Ten

The list as a device is explicitly utilised as a methodology for interactive documentary by Brasier. It reappears in Payne's chapter about a blog and video compilation by Alexander Hahn, Keen's use of indexing in documentary design, and Frankham's locative, dialogical trail making. The list, as several note, is sympathetic to the encyclopaedic and procedural abilities of computers and databases and, as a consequence, well suited to provide an architecture that is open ended and ongoing. Lists, after all, are as long as they need to be, encourage addition, can be about anything, and carry within them their own principle of structure. In this way lists are an alternative to story as once we have a list we then concern ourselves with imagining possible relations and relevance between the things listed.

For the authors here who utilise lists and list making, noticing comes to matter as a method to curate and triage the things being listed. Noticing here becomes a habit of addressing oneself toward the world that listing facilitates, inviting a manner of openness toward things that is unlike the imperative of narrative because listing does not experience an obligation of explanation or account. As Brasier, Frankham, and Payne all note, while documentary can rely on narrative to justify why and how what is shown matters, when we rely on a list compiled by noticing—in the absence of the scaffolding of narrative—different relations to the world are invited of us.

Eleven

All contributors also note a change in scale in media practice, and in the artefacts that are the product of these new practices. This change of scale is evident in the use of a smart phone for film making as we see in Schleser's *24Frames 24Hours*, the fragments from Marker's *Sunless* that Brasier uses in her experimental recomposition, the videographic asides that Payne documents, Keen's call for a sketch practice, Frankham's speculations about a location-based media, and my own interest in the informal media trails we now leave in our wake.

The sketch, perhaps even more so than the list, also recurs and is a marker of what can be characterised as "post-monument" media. Monumental media is the sort of media that is careful to maintain professional or broadcast standards, is protective of industry conventions, and seeks to maximise its audience. Its hallmarks are craft expertise emphasised through the industrial application of technical specialisation, equipment, and distribution channels. Documentary has its own counter-traditions and practices that often fall outside of this monumentality, making it a point of honour to use minimal crews and lightweight equipment to make work with sketch-like qualities. Seminal figures such as Rouch, Varda, and Marker easily fall under this banner. This affinity between documentary and sketching is then advantageous as it suggests an agility and nimbleness that is well suited to interactive documentary, as Keen notes. (As an aside, this might also help account for the seemingly ready adoption of interactivity and networks by documentary compared to narrative cinema.)

Twelve

When things are small scale, composed as lists, and sketched, then the facilitating and enabling of relations between media becomes important. Small things are easier to place next to other small things, particularly when they are never fixed in place. This is present throughout each chapter as, in turn and in their own manner, it is a relational practice or system that is eventually being described. This lets us see that as documentary moves slowly and more deeply into a post-industrial and post-monumental media we are seeing that the role of new interactive systems is to enable relational practices with relational machines.

THIRTEEN

Taken together the qualities of listing, noticing, sketching, scale, and relationality show how affordable digital tools, combined with a near-to-hand network, have allowed for varieties of nonfiction media making that are an everyday noticing that complements our documentary heritage. These digital tools and networks allow these qualities and practices to emerge and how the works described here are made up of ambient, small, observations, what might be considered to be almost asides, allows for a postmonumental nonfiction media making to emerge.

The rise of these new practices and machines as the shadow—or allure—of digitisation, computers, and the World Wide Web as a socio-technical network is, I hope, what this anthology contributes to the study and development of interactive documentary. YMMV.

BIBLIOGRAPHY

Andrew Murphie. Making Sense: The Transformation of Documentary by Digital and Networked Media. *Studies in Documentary Film* 8.3 (2014): 188–204.

Deleuze, Gilles, and Félix Guattari. *Kafka: Towards a Minor Literature*. Trans. Dana Polan and Réda Bensmaïa. Minneapolis: University of Minnesota Press, 1986.

van Dijck, Jose. *Mediated Memories in the Digital Age*. Stanford: Stanford University Press, 2007.

Dovey, Jonathan. "Dinosaurs and Butterflies – Media Practice Research in New Media Ecologies". *Journal of Media Practice* 9.3 (2008): 243–256.

Geertz, Clifford. "Thick Description: Toward an Interpretive Theory of Culture". *The Interpretation of Cultures*. New York: Basic Books, 1977. 3–30.

Grainge, Paul. *Ephemeral Media: Transitory Screen Culture from Television to YouTube*. Basingstoke: British Film Institute, 2011.

Haraway, Donna. "Situated Knowledges: The Science Question in Feminism and the Privilege of Partial Perspective". *Feminist Studies* 14.3 (1988): 575–599.

Ponterotto, Joseph G. "Brief Note on the Origins, Evolution, and Meaning of the Qualitative Research Concept "Thick Description"". *The Qualitative Report* 11.3 (2006): 538–549.

Weinberger, David. *Small Pieces Loosely Joined: A Unified Theory of the Web*. New York: Perseus Books, 2002.

Moments of Noticing: 'I See You' as a Speculative Work Towards an Essayistic List Practice for Interactive Documentary

Hannah Brasier

Abstract This chapter uses an interactive film as a case study to argue for list making as an alternative to stories for making interactive documentaries. It argues that lists are suited to network-specific media forms because lists are made up of discrete parts that can be easily arranged in multiple ways. This raises the problem of how makers and audiences might understand lists and the chapter details how this has been explored in the case study.

Keywords interactive documentary • essay film • noticing • lists

Introduction

This chapter considers an online video essay, called *I See You* (Brasier 2014), that I made in the context of my project-based research. *I See You* explores a method of making interactive documentary that is specifically multilinear. As multilinear projects are made up of semi-autonomous

H. Brasier (✉)
College of Design and Social Context, RMIT University,
Melbourne, VIC, Australia

A. Miles (ed.), *Digital Media and Documentary*,
https://doi.org/10.1007/978-3-319-68643-1_2

elements that are able to be connected to numerous other elements, how can we make nonfiction works for and with this environment? To explore this question a methodology of listing to notice was adopted in *I See You*. This is a project that notices and lists individual moments in Marker's essay film *Sunless* (1983). By adapting the method of ordinary noticing, marking, and recording from Mason's *Researching your Own Practice: The Discipline of Noticing* (2002), combined with a practice of listing, I heuristically developed a multilinear nonfiction practice of noticing that can be used for documentary. This chapter discusses *I See You* in light of the methods in which it was made, and the contextual underpinnings of the essay film and the list as a method that allows an interactive essayist mode of documentary to emerge. Through making and contextualising *I See You*, noticing and the list become a way to pay attention to, and organise video content, in a way that maintains the individuality and openness of footage in a multilinear manner. When viewing *I See You* the user is encouraged to re-enact this noticing and listing, through interaction, because the content, pattern, and interface of the work invites this type of engagement.

What *I See You* Is

I See You (Brasier 2014) consists of thirty-seven video clips of up to ten seconds in length, selected from *Sunless*. These individual clips are organised using Korsakow, which is an "open-source application … for the authoring of database narratives: primarily documentaries" (Soar 2014, 154). Interactive films made using Korsakow are colloquially known as "K-films," and K–films are a database of video content that is organised by a film-maker using keywords to create patterns of relations between the video content. An example of how a K-film works can be seen in Soar's *Ceci N'est Pas Embres* where the clip database of the film contains thirty-four individual edited videos from Soar's sabbatical with his family in a small country town in Southwest France (2012). The main keywords Soar attributed to these clips are Winter, Spring and Summer, and the user moves through these seasonal clips as they progress through the interactive documentary. The interface regularly changes, although generally there is one larger video playing in a window and two or more smaller thumbnail videos that the user may choose from to open as the next playing video (Soar 2012). In most K-films, like Soar's *Ceci N'est Pas Embres*, a user interacts with the work through this interface as it allows the user to view and navigate the videos in its database, subject to the constraints authored by the film-maker. The relationship between the videos, the patterns they form, and the interface of a K-film largely reflects Manovich's understanding of new media work "as the construction of an interface to a database" (Manovich, 226). The patterns of a K-Film consist of the visual and thematic relationships that emerge between the individual clips, and these are determined by the keywords given to each of the video clips. Generally in K-films an interface is made up of one main video and a set of accompanying thumbnails. The main video is the video clip currently playing, and the thumbnails provide access to open another main video.

Content

The thirty-seven video clips that make up the content of *I See You* are the shots and sequences I noticed, more than others, through repeated viewings of *Sunless*. The main images noticed consisted of faces, animals, crowds, and the images transformed in what the female narrator of *Sunless* calls "the zone." *I See You* contains eleven face, fourteen animal, eight crowd, and four zone clips, each with the sound removed. The face shots are predominantly close-ups of a single person or animal, for example, the close-up of a woman's face as she naps on a train in Tokyo, and a close-up of an owl blinking. The crowd clips are largely wide shots, for example, pedestrians crossing a road in Tokyo, a queue of commuters validating tickets at a train station, and businessmen walking through a darkened electronics mall. The clips of animals vary in style, ranging from a wide shot of a water bird reflected on a lake, a medium shot of an emu prancing along a path, to a close-up sequence of different deer on television. The four zone clips visually reinterpret earlier footage used in *Sunless* in an electronic synthesised environment. For instance, the clip of an emu prancing is reinterpreted in "the zone" in *Sunless*, and is also reused as a clip in the database of *I See You*.

There are clips within *I See You* that exceed the single categories of face, animal, crowd, or zone. These clips are multifaceted because they show more than one category, for example, the close-up of the owl's face blinking is a face and an animal. Another example of a multifaceted clip is the sequence of shots showing rows of white Japanese cat sculptures beckoning to us with one paw raised, which is animal and crowd. Clips from "the zone" are less abundant in *I See You* as they reinterpret animals, face, and crowds from earlier in *Sunless*.

Pattern

The patterns that emerge in *I See You* largely reflect how I have categorised clips through the keywords of face, animal, crowd, and zone. Keywords in Korsakow allow clips with common characteristics to form clusters, and those clips that I have described as multifaceted have more than one keyword so they can act as bridges, linking the different clusters. Soar, when describing the making of his *Ceci N'est Pas Embres* (2012) calls these bridges "pinchpoint" clips because they allow the K-film to transition from one keyword cluster to another (Soar 2014). A pinchpoint clip in *I See You* is the earlier example of the face of the owl, which links from the face cluster to the animal cluster because it has the "face" and "animal" keywords applied. As a result, when a user interacts with *I See You*, the film moves between these clusters of faces, crowds, and animals, and eventually arrives at the zone. The film randomly begins with any of the clips within the database, and the user, through their choices, will then move in and out of the different clusters in a variable and multilinear manner. While the connections between clips are loose, they are constrained by the keywords and so the "order of the scenes is calculated while viewing" (Thalhofer 2015). Without these multifaceted pinchpoints to bridge between clusters a user would find themselves caught within clusters of similar clips with no way to navigate or find connection to the other clusters that make up *I See You*. The patterns formed between clips by keywords are supported by how many "lives" each clip has in the K-film. The lives attribute in Korsakow constrains how many times an individual clip can be played, and in *I See You* each animal, crowd, and face clip has two lives, whilst zone clips have infinite lives.

In addition, Korsakow allows a weighting to be applied to individual clips that affects their likelihood of being found and so shown to a user. A higher weighting makes a clip more likely to appear, a lower weighting less likely. In *I See You* the zone clips have a low weighting so they are less likely to appear in the film compared to the animal, crowd, and face clips. By providing animal, crowd, and face clips with two lives, and infinite lives with a lowered weighting to the zone clips, as the user interacts with the film they are more likely to see animal, crowd, and face clips, which will then disappear as they can only be viewed twice, eventually leaving the user in a looping circle of the four clips that make up the zone cluster. Once the user has selected a zone clip from the thumbnails they are unable to return to any of the other clusters during that particular viewing because the clips in the zone only provide keyword matches with each other. Hence, as in *Sunless*, when the user enters the zone cluster a sort of end point is provided for *I See You* and the infinite lives attributed to the four clips allows them to continually loop amongst themselves, until the user decides to leave.

Interface

As the user interacts with *I See You*, the clusters of faces, crowds, animals, and zone can be identified through the relationships between the currently playing video and the thumbnails visible in the interface. In *I See You* the interface uses a white background with three black and white thumbnails (buttons) and one colour main video, arranged horizontally, across the centre of the browser window. There is generally a thematic similarity between what is playing in the current video and the black and white thumbnails. For instance, the main video might be a clip of a group of businessmen and women crossing a street in Tokyo, and the thumbnails could show commuters hurrying down steps, a woman looking back with a queue of people behind her, and a crowd of people walking towards the camera in a wintery Tokyo. After selecting one of these thumbnails, and finding more shots of crowds, a user will ideally notice, perhaps after several more choices, that they are watching different iterations of crowds. Further, the position of the video that is playing is related to its cluster. For instance, the animal cluster plays video in the first video position from the left, faces in the second, crowd the third, and when you enter the zone the clip will open and play in the right of the list. This interface design reinforces the way the clips are themed into clusters, helping orientate the user's attention toward noticing what things there are in common between the shots based on their content. This combination of content, patterns, and interface creates the interactive visual essay that is *I See You*, consisting of moments of what I noticed of *Sunless.*

Noticing and *I See You*

I See You emerges from a method of attuned noticing I have adopted from Mason's *Researching Your Own Practice: The Discipline of Noticing* (2002). In this way *I See You* can be seen to reflect Mason's three categories of "ordinary noticing," "marking," and "recording." These three forms of noticing have been realised in *I See You* through the use of lists as a way to evaluate whether noticing is a viable strategy for an interactive, essayist mode of documentary.

Ordinary noticing was the first step in making *I See You*. Mason describes ordinary noticing as making a "distinction, to create foreground and background, to distinguish some 'thing' from its surroundings" (2002, 33). Ordinary noticing in making *I See You* involved watching *Sunless* numerous times and noting what things distinguished themselves above others. For each viewing I would write a new list of noticed things. The first viewings produced broad and general lists of ordinary noticing, for example, simply noting a quote, an image, and recording the time code. These lists of ordinary noticing became, as Bogost notes, "lists of objects without explication," which served to then draw my "attention toward them [the listed things] with greater attentiveness" (45). The aim of this ordinary noticing through list-making was to see what my attention was being drawn to in *Sunless.*

This ordinary noticing provided the basis to recognise overall themes in what I noticed and so my lists became more focused. This is Mason's second form of noticing: marking. For Mason marking "signals that there was something salient about the incident" and is a step up from ordinary noticing because you not only "notice but you are able to initiate mention of what you have noticed" (33). Mason further indicates "*marking* is a heightened form of noticing" (33). Marking allowed me to draw connections between the moments of ordinary noticing, and afforded me the ability to cluster items under larger headings such as trains, watching, memory, and religion. By iteratively and reflexively practicing marking I collected noticed moments into clusters under the larger themes of faces, animals, crowds, and zone, which became the terms used in the final version of *I See You*. These lists of faces, animals, crowds, and zone, as marked items, then became prompts in a second iteration of noticing while viewing *Sunless.* In this second viewing I collected short sequences or shots of faces, animals, crowds, and zone for use in *I See You*. This process of ordinary noticing leading through marking to clustering items reflects Bogost's claim that the list "involves cataloguing things, but also drawing attention to the coupling of chasms between them" (50). Through keywording, images of faces, animals, and crowds are catalogued into content-based lists. The lists of marked things were in turn marked through keywords in Korsakow, creating a catalogue based on noticing. Thus, what listing does as a method in *I See You* is use ordinary noticing and marking to maintain the autonomy of things, simultaneous with accounting for their resonances, without fixing their similarities into static relations. This autonomy and open togetherness of the list is what *I See You* does, and what K-Films allow for more generally.

Finally, Mason regards recording as the final step toward a practice of "disciplined" noticing. Recording involves making a "brief-but-vivid note of some incident" where "you both externalise it from your immediate flow of thoughts, and you give yourself access to it at a later date, for further analysis" (34). *I See You* is this act of recording for me, as it is how I externalised and provided myself access to the individual moments of my noticing of *Sunless.* By removing clips from *Sunless* and placing them into Korsakow I could iteratively prototype interface designs, exporting, and evaluating the film in progress to confirm if the patterns being created through the keywords in *I See You* reflected what I noticed. The interface of *I See You* as a horizontal list developed from recognising the significance of listing to noticing, and therefore wanting the work to reflect the list-making processes taken to make *I See You.* Through this list interface the user makes lists through their interaction with the work. Similarly, each step of ordinary noticing, marking, and recording used lists as a method to attune my attention to what I was noticing, and provided a viable method to generate lists for use in an interactive K-film. This method of noticing through listing, from watching *Sunless* to making *I See You,* can be realised as an approach for collecting footage for further multilinear documentary projects. Listing to notice could be used to attune attention to things in the world as a method for interactive documentary projects interested in observation.

Contextual Underpinnings of *I See You*

I See You shows and then invites users to list through interaction the patterns of, faces, crowds, and animals that is different to Marker's rendering of them in *Sunless.* However, whether or not the listing of *I See You* offers a basis for an essayist mode of interactive documentary needs consideration of the qualities of the essay film and the list, to think about how the characteristics of each are realised in *I See You.*

The essay film is described by theorists such as Corrigan and Rascaroli as films that present thoughts and ideas filtered through a strong subjective voice. Corrigan defines essay films as having a "tripartite structure of subjectivity, public experience, and thinking" (63) where essay films "ask viewers to experience the world … as the mediated encounter of thinking through the world, as a world experienced through a thinking mind" (35). The essay film constructs a space for thinking by filmmaker and audience through its use of form and content, where we witness a subject in the act of thinking through their concerns. Similarly, as Rascaroli notes, the "temporal, spatial and critical distance between voice and subject matter" (55) allows essay films to "distance themselves from their images and scrutinise them, almost 'finding' and presenting them anew, as pre-existing objects" (52). What essay films do is express the process of thinking through the materiality of film, using sound, images, and edits, to allow the viewer to think *with* the essayist as they think through and about their images.

What I propose is that lists developed through noticing are a structuring device that provides a simple vehicle for such essayistic thinking in interactive documentary. This conception of lists as a structure emerges from Bogost who considers lists as "provocations, as litanies of surprising contrasted curiosities" (38), and Eco, who in the *Infinity of Lists* provides explanations and examples of lists from the history of literature and art. Eco describes lists as infinite, using Homer's catalogue of ships in the *Iliad* as an example where the writer is faced "with something that is immensely large, or unknown, of which we still do not know enough or of which we shall never know, the author proposes a list as a specimen, example, or indication, leaving the reader to imagine the rest" (49). For Eco, the list is then a "form of representation [which] suggests infinity almost *physically*, because in fact *it does not end*, nor does it conclude in form" (17). In addition, the list eschews narrative and, as an infinite set of items, a list can be reorganised in many different ways producing a multiplicity of versions and interpretations. This clearly has affinities to the multilinearity evident in interactive documentary.

Bogost suggests that lists draw attention to things, as "lists of objects without explication can do the philosophical work of drawing our attention toward them with greater attentiveness" (45). For Eco the "list becomes a way of reshuffling the world ... to accumulate properties in order to bring out new relationships between distant things" (327). Frankham positions Eco's idea of the list's ability to reshuffle the world as a model for poetic documentary because lists offer "a formal approach that also speaks of the infinite possibilities of combining and making connections across a networked field of elements" (138). Frankham uses Shonagon's "lists of rare things, splendid things, worthless things and things that quicken the heart" (146) in *The Pillow Book* (2006) as an example of how lists can be poetic. Frankham goes on to suggest that the "quality of her [Shonagon's] world and a glimpse of her mind are evoked through both the items that each list gathers and the topics under which they are assembled" (147). By utilising the list in Frankham's poetic documentary, a viewer is encouraged to notice the multiple possible connections between the array of images offered.

Combining Bogost, Eco, and Frankham's descriptions of what lists do provides an understanding of lists as a viable structural device to gather, and draw attention to, individual items that have been noticed. Each individual item on a list remains separate to the others for, as Bogost notes, items on a list are not concretely joined, rather they are "loosely joined … by the gentle knot of a comma" (38). The relationship between each item in a list can be shuffled and reorganised in innumerable ways to provide various, and potentially infinite meanings, and interpretations. Further, the looseness of the relationship between listed items for Frankham "facilitate[s] spaces for engagement and openness of interpretation … that permits a sense of cohesion at the same time as it increases the gap between project elements" (138). The list can therefore provide, as a structural device in interactive documentary practice, the potential to expand the space between the elements of content, interactivity, and interface. This becomes a space where maker and user select individual elements, thereby changing and producing multiple relations between these elements. If an essay film requires authorial presence realised through voice and image, then the list provides a method for interactive documentary by exploiting the space between these elements as an open space of thinking.

I See You performs as a list of the highlights I noticed, and expands the space between these noticed moments by removing them from the rapid pace of Marker's editing, where images "fly quickly before us … things land before us, only to be quickly launched, flipped, scooted, pushed and removed" (Mavor, 747). *I See You* is about demonstrating the moments of noticing as a way of list making for interactive documentary, and is less then an analysis of *Sunless*. As a practice of attuned noticing and listing *I See You* shows what I noticed of *Sunless*, and organises these observations in Korsakow to list these observations into clusters to emphasise these moments further. Even those clips that are a sequence, rather than single shots, concentrate on the discreteness of a moment, as the sequences are lists of one thing repeated, for instance, the three shots of deer on television. These moments of noticing, gathered into lists that make patterns, are the basis of *I See You* where I have made a list of what I have noticed without the presence of an explicit authorial voice to guide the journey through the work. However, in *I See You* there is no strong subjective voice that is one of the tripartite qualities of authorial presence, voice, and image that make up the essay film.

What seems to have happened in *I See You* is a figuration of voice outside of the subjective thinking aloud of the essayist in the essay film. In the case of *I See You*, voice is evident in its keyword formed constraints, giving the work its list-making structure. The strong subjective voice of the essayist, therefore, does not seem to find a place in multilinear documentaries that pay attention to the things of the world, rather voice is achieved subtly in what attention is being drawn to in the relations between clips. The list-like structure and the interface design draw the user's attention toward the individual visual moments of an owl blinking or a woman napping, whilst drawing the user's attention through the interface to the resonances between this clip and the others around it. The user then selects a new clip according to their own individual patterns of noticing contributing their voice through choice and interaction.

The Network and *I See You*

In response to the need to develop methods of making and structuring interactive documentaries that recognise the network and multilinearity as the site of practice, *I See You* is an interactive list film that emphasises moments of deliberate noticing. In "Interactive Documentary and Affective Ecologies" Miles notes that the "distribution of documentary online is not synonymous with the deeper implications of the network as a site of practice, a site that produces its own habitat and ecology of media artefacts" (81). How can we make documentary films that recognise the network as a specific site of practice? And what are the differences between networked and traditional documentary practice that matter?

If we compare *Sunless* to *I See You* we can see what some of the implications of the networked environment are. In *Sunless* the relationship between shots, sequences, and sound is stable because as viewers we see the same sequence of shots with the same soundtrack over the same one-hundred-minute duration on every viewing. We may notice new things on different viewings, as I did through my iterative noticing as I made *I See You*, however, the order, pace, and length of *Sunless* is fixed and unchanging.

In contrast, when making *I See You* I constrained the possible relations between clips by the use of keywords that the Korsakow system uses to find matches and I did not edit fixed sequences. This difference between fixed and potential relations is elaborated upon by Miles, who considers a main transition from linear to interactive online video occurs when "hard connections usually formed between parts are now soft and multiple" (72). In *I See You* the Korsakow software chooses three thumbnails from all the possible connections available from the clip currently playing, and the user then chooses which one of these three thumbnails they want to open and watch. This is further "softened" as the system can and does choose different thumbnails to provide possible connections from the same video each time a user interacts with the work. Obviously, the decisions made by the system are constrained by the keywords I have used, for example, if the main video playing is the montage of deer on television then the three thumbnails chosen by the Korsakow system will all belong to the "animal" keyword group. The "softness" that Miles describes comes from how the system selects these three clips out of the fifteen clips in *I See You* that have the "animal" keyword. This softness of the Korsakow system therefore allows one clip to have numerous and changing connections or relations with other clips.

These relations between clips in *I See You* are unfixed, loose, and multiple, and the duration of the film is now dependent upon how long the user wants to watch each clip before clicking away, and varies depending on when a zone clip becomes accessible and is selected by a user. This is highly dependent on the journey each user takes through the work, influenced by the selections made by Korsakow and their thumbnail choices. *I See You* therefore has a length that is dependent on how long the user wishes to watch each clip, how long they wish to watch the work, and if they stay with *I See You* the speed it takes for them to click into the zone, and then how long they decide to spend there. The softness of shot order and duration in *I See You* differs then from the fixed linearity and duration of *Sunless*.

As the maker of *I See You*, I chose the parts of *Sunless* that would make up the database content, wrote the constraints of the work by deciding on the keywords, lives, and clip ratings making up the pattern of the work, and designed the interface layout. However, I did not edit together a fixed sequence of shots a user would watch over a specific time length. This change of position from an editor of fixed sequences to an architect of navigation in interactive documentary is described by Brush where "much of interactive documentary is really just a new editorial process" (n.p.). My position as a documentary film-maker has then moved from creating a fixed sequence of shots that a viewer watches unfold over a certain period of time to creating loose connections between clips, including the potential to make a K-film that has no fixed duration. In terms of moving documentary practice from a linear to a multilinear environment the role of the film-maker has now moved "from determining fixed relations between shots to assembling particular sets of possible relations" (Miles, 75). The particular sets of possible relations in *I See You* are formed by the keyword groups of face, animal, crowds, and zone, with pinchpoint clips allowing for connections and user movement between each cluster.

Implications of the Network

An implication, then, of *I See You* in relation to the network is a multiplicity of relations where "multiplicity is a result of what is known as granularity and facetted relations" (Miles, 73). Granularity describes the extent to which something can be broken down into smaller parts and still retain sense, while facetted relations describes the way that each of these smaller parts provides "many faces of possible connection" (Miles, 75). Miles uses blogs as an example of a highly granular form because a blog's "minimal unit, the post, exhibits a high degree of closure where I can read a blog post and understand it without usually having to read what comes before, or after, in that blog" (74). From this, Miles considers a medium to be highly granular "if it is made up of small parts that are self-contained to the extent that they make sense by themselves as is" (74). In *I See You* each clip is a moment that is understandable in itself, is not telling a narrative, and so the clips exhibit a high degree of granularity.

Facetted relations in *I See You* are achieved through the keywords I have attributed to the clips. In other words, keywords allow multiple relations between the clips within each cluster and each clip therefore has multiple faces of connection amongst themselves. For example, there are eight clips that have the "crowd" keyword, and therefore each clip within this cluster has the potential to connect to any one of these other eight clips. These granular clips organised into clusters through common keywords affords the multilinearity evident in *I See You*.

Parallels Between Lists, Essay Films, and Implications of the Network

A question that emerges from *I See You* as a multilinear film is how the aesthetic qualities of lists and the essay combine with facetted relations, granularity, and multiplicity, to allow for an interactive documentary practice. A provisional answer is that essay films using lists provide a productive model for interactive documentary practice. Web-specific work seems to desire content that is granular and able to be used in multiple contexts. Lists support this as they are highly granular, consisting of separate and individual items (Bogost, 38) that can be reshuffled, and continually added to or removed. As Frankham notes, in lists the "relationship between parts is kept loose" (138).

A further way in which essay and list-making practices align with granularity and facetted relations is how lists and the essay are often positioned as non-narrative forms. Manovich, for example, contrasts narrative to web-based structures and finds it surprising that "narratives—still exist in new media" when there is "nothing in the logic of the medium itself that would foster its generation" (228). For Manovich, narrative is not part of the logic of databases and the web. Non-narrative forms such as lists and essay films, as in the case of *I See You,* then appear as models for interactive documentary that relies on databases and the web. In this conception, non-narrative becomes any form organised by structures that do not rely on narratological cause and effect relationships. Corrigan and White, for instance, consider "lists, repetition, or contrasts" (263) as examples of structures that can be used in non-narrative documentary, using Keaton's *Heaven* (1987) as an example that uses the list as a non-narrative organising device. *Heaven* presents a "litany of faces and voices to answer such questions as 'Does heaven exist?' and 'Is there sex in heaven?'" that is "better understood as a playful list of unpredictable reactions to the possibility of the life hereafter," rather than a "religious mystery tale" (Corrigan and White, 264). In other words, in *Heaven,* list-making allows multiple responses to the idea of heaven, thus avoiding any single or definitive statement about what heaven is. Listing then allows for a non-narrative structure as the form presents multiple ideas as opposed to a single and closed trajectory of thought. The list for Corrigan and White tends to "eschew or de-emphasise stories and narratives" (263) and so is viable as a method for making and structuring non-narrative documentary.

The multiplicity of perspectives allowed by the list structure of *Heaven* is a quality common to many essay films, and the open-ended nature of the list, combined with the simple manner in which lists eschew genre (we can make lists of anything) makes the list well suited to networked essay films that then do not need to rely upon narrative as an organisational principle. To quote Chanan "the essay film is documentary at its freest, favouring symbolic and associative thinking over narrative" (27), while Corrigan notes that thoughts "shape and direct the film, often complicating traditional narrative" (30). Corrigan further considers the essayistic persona to be "analogously fragmented and unstable" (31), and there are obvious parallels between such fragmentation and instability and the granularity and facetted relations of the network. Essay films emphasise subjective thinking and the expression of ideas over narrative trajectories and *I See You* explores lists as a way to make multilinear essay films. *I See You* experiments with the viability of lists as an essayist method and finds that lists are well suited to the granular and open forms of network-specific software such as Korsakow.

Conclusion

Through making *I See You* and reflecting on the finished K-Film in relation to the essay film and multilinearity, listing to notice emerges as a directed form of attuned noticing. In this attuned noticing authorial voice is now rendered outside of a literal speaking voice into the list-like arrangement of video images through the pattern and interface of the work. The faces, crowds, and animals that are materialised through the listing process became moments worth noticing, and these were then used in *I See You* to make lists with. Listing to notice softly achieves an authorial subjectivity simply in what is noticed and this then allows the user to think about the space between the things listed. In other words because the user can pause the work by not clicking, they have time to potentially notice the patterns I have noticed as well as their own patterns through their own form of directed noticing. There is no explicit narrating what this pattern is, although it does become apparent in the repetition of similar images across the interface that the user may notice, as they attune to the rhythms of *I See You,* through deliberate acts of watching, noticing and clicking. Another outcome of the use of the list is its ability to maintain the granular openness of multilinear network systems like Korsakow. The list then provides a distinctively multilinear approach to noticing that then subtly achieves an essayistic voice in what is perceived. As *Sunless* was used to test listing to notice as a methodology, a question emerges about how directed noticing, listing, and filming fragments engages with the world as a non-fiction practice?

Bibliography

Bogost, Ian. *Alien Phenomenology. Or What It's Like to Be a Thing*. Minneapolis: University of Minnesota Press, 2012.

Braiser, Hannah (dir.). *I See You*. Korsakow Film, 2014, Web.

Brasier, Hannah. "Interface Development. Vertical and Horizontal Lists. Infinite and Finite Lists." *Hannah Brasier*, March 6, 2014, Web.

Brush, Jason. "How Interactivity Is Evolving the Documentary." *DOX European Documentary Magazine,* no. 102, September, 2014, Web.

Chanan, Michael. "The Role of History in the Individual: Working Notes for a Film." *The Cinema of Me: The Self and Subjectivity in First Person Documentary*. Ed. Alisa Lebow. New York: Columbia University Press, 2012. 15–32.

Corrigan, Timothy. *The Essay Film: From Montaigne, After Marker*. Oxford: Oxford University Press, 2011.

Corrigan, Timothy, and Patricia White. *The Film Experience: An Introduction*. 3rd ed. Boston: Bedford/St. Martin's, 2012.

Eco, Umberto. *The Infinity of Lists*. New York: Rizzoli, 2009.

Frankham, Bettina Louise. "A Poetic Approach to Documentary: Discomfort of Form, Rhetorical Strategies and Aesthetic Experience." Dissertation, University of Technology Sydney, 2013.

Keaton, Diane (dir.). *Heaven*, Island Pictures, 1987.

Manovich, Lev. *The Language of New Media*. Cambridge: Massachusetts Institute of Technology Press, 2001.

Marker, Chris (dir.). *Sunless*, Argos Films, 1983.

Mason, John. *Researching Your Own Practice: The Discipline of Noticing*. London: Routledge Falmer, 2002.

Mavor, Carol. "Happiness with a Long Piece of Black Leader: Chris Marker's Sunless." *Art History* 30.5 (2007): 738–756.

Miles, Adrian. "Interactive Documentary and Affective Ecologies." *New Documentary Ecologies: Emerging Platforms, Practices and Discourses*. Ed. Kate Nash, Craig Hight and Catherine Summerhayes. London: Palgrave Macmillan, 2014. 67–82.

Rascaroli, Laura. *The Personal Camera: Subjective Cinema and the Essay Film*. London: Wallflower Press, 2009.

Shonagon, Sei. *The Pillow Book*. Trans. Meredith McKinney. London: Penguin Group, 2006.

Soar, Matt (dir.). *Ceci N'est Pas Embres.* Korsakow Film, 2012, Web.

Soar, Matt. "Making (with) the Korsakow System: Database Documentaries as Articulation and Assembly." *New Documentary Ecologies: Emerging Platforms, Practices and Discourses.* Ed. Kate Nash, Craig Hight and Catherine Summerhayes. London: Palgrave Macmillan, 2014. 154–173.

Thalhofer, Florian. "About." *KORSAKOW: Dynamic Storytelling.* March, 2015, Web.

Documentary, Instructions, and Experiences of Place

Bettina Frankham

Abstract This chapter describes the concept for a documentary that is also an instruction-based artwork. As a mobile, site-specific, and screen-based locative project the intention is that the embodied experience of the digital content is emphasized, setting up a resonance between content, instructions, the user and the real world. The objective of this method is to guide the audience as a participant through a series of directed poetic experiences to provoke situated knowledges about place and to consider other perspectives.

Keywords: experience • instructions • polyvocality • participatory • locative media • mobile media • augmented reality • walking practice

Finding Ways—I

> Find a public place to sit that has a good view of people moving around.
> Pick out one person from the people going past.
> Follow them with your eyes, watching the path they take and where they go.
> Try to be subtle. Look away if they notice you.
> [*How would you feel if they noticed you?*]

B. Frankham (✉)
School of Communication, Faculty of Arts and Social Sciences, University of Technology Sydney, Ultimo, NSW, Australia

A. Miles (ed.), *Digital Media and Documentary*,
https://doi.org/10.1007/978-3-319-68643-1_3

Are there any clues that might help you guess at their story?
Think about their life and the web of people they are connected to.
See in your mind's eye a network of possible variables: linkages, conflicts, pasts, futures, hopes, dreams, secrets, deceptions, disappointments, and tragedies all exploding out from this one person walking by.
Dwell in this web of who they might be for roughly seven heartbeats.
[*Are you counting heartbeats or thinking about this person?*
Can you do both at the same time?]
Now pick another person, someone who catches your eye, and repeat the game.
Continue until the landscape before you is thick with the traces of overlapping paths and networks of interlinking lives connecting across time and space.
Think about the assumptions, contexts, histories, prejudices, and values that shaped your conjectures.
Sit with that examination for a bit to see if it starts to prickle at your soul.
This is where we begin.

Introduction

My introduction sounds like a familiar refrain…

> Innovations in technology and consequent shifts in how we engage with media objects are prompting the need to rethink how we conceive of screen-based documentary. While the traditional forms of linear film and video documentary are being broken up for online delivery—fragmented, networked, made non-linear—there is also considerable potential to expand the documentary experience beyond customary understandings of the screen. (*Frankham, in an early draft of this essay*)

More than a breathless anticipation or celebration of all that is new, technological and user-generated (just because it is new, technological and user-generated), this is a call to rethink what the practice of documentary can be in the changing contexts of production, distribution, exhibition, and participation within which we find ourselves. With expanded methods of media gathering, interaction, and non-linearity have come questions about the generic conventions of documentary practice. Questions arise of whether these new approaches to production, content creation, curation, delivery, and consumption constitute a transformation so great that we are no longer talking about documentary per se but some other entity that is still coming into being.

Even so, there does seem to be a set of behaviours, intentions, and methods that are returned to as a core of what gets called documentary practice. The John Grierson-attributed definition of documentary as "the creative treatment of actuality" (Grierson and Hardy 1979, 11) springs to mind as does Michael Renov's "four fundamental tendencies of documentary" that are the impulses to record, reveal or preserve; persuade or promote; analyse or interrogate; and to express (1993, 21), with a fifth *ethical* function added later (2007, 23). Debated, embroidered, augmented, contested, yet nonetheless returned to, these principles are valued as points of definition and resistance that we can push against in discussions of what documentary is and what it may yet become.

Considerations of the affordances and constraints associated with digital platforms and systems are valuable in moving this discussion forward, as are thoughts of how these platforms and systems may interact with already established documentary processes. It is already well established through the work of theorists such as Renov (2004) and Bill Nichols (2010) that documentary knowledge can be generated through a range of representational methods beyond the presentation of facts. For example, in a description of the performative mode of documentary, Nichols tells of how "embodied knowledge provides entry into an understanding of the more general processes at work in society" (201). This inclusion of the subjective, affective, and perceptual dimensions of knowing leads me to consider the different kinds of embodied and experiential *source material* that can be mustered in support of a broad understanding of documentary rhetorical strategies. Approaches to time and visual style, resonances between media and location, and the circumstances of spectatorship, all produce their own kinds of embodied knowledge that impact on the experience of the documentary that is in addition to the content of a project.

This chapter explores the possibilities and limitations of framing a location-specific documentary practice. This practice is formulated as a series of instructions developed from interviews with people who have a strong relationship with a chosen location. This is, currently, an imagined, speculative project, entitled *Finding Ways*. The intent of the *Finding Ways* project is to make layers of material (instructions, interview material, archival images, audience contributions) available via GPS-enabled mobile phones along specific sections of the coastline near Wollongong (New South Wales) called the Blue Mile. The instructions operate as prompts to set up opportunities for audience participants to respond with text, images, video, and sound that can then be reseeded into the landscape as additional location-specific media. As a socially engaged locative media documentary, the intention of *Finding Ways* is to strike resonances between the physical location and the media experienced there, so that both are augmented by the interaction, potentially prompting shifts in preconceptions and a movement away from understandings that are monolithic and singular. The concept of *Finding Ways* relies then on an expanded notion of documentary that starts from the idea of documentary as an impulse to produce experiences with rhetorical effects.

Interspersed throughout this chapter are numbered sections entitled Finding Ways that are the instructions for one method to develop a locative media documentary. As descriptions of a process, they are intended to provide some insight to the thinking, and motivation, behind this imagined project. As textual instruction, they work as examples of how a sense of the instructor (the human source of the instructions) can leak into the otherwise procedural form and content of an instruction-based documentary. These instructions serve to reinforce an argument that instructions are not neutral, but arise from a subjectivity and serve to shape a view of the world.

Expanded Fields—Documentary as an Experience in Itself

One of my ongoing research interests is exploring poetic approaches to documentary making. These poetic methods tend to work at the edges of what might be recognisable as documentary, however, a poetic approach is edifying in the way it can highlight the rhetorical impact of the aesthetic choices made within documentary practice more broadly. In this regard, these poetic approaches can be considered as an intersectional practice, in the way that it applies methods from artistic and documentary disciplines. I take this intersectionality as a cue to explore scholarly research relevant to visual and media arts practices, as well as scholarship that is focused on traditional and emerging forms of documentary.

A poetic approach within linear documentary is frequently characterised by an openness of form that enables moments of pause and contemplation. In these works, an affective and aesthetic encounter with the film is the primary means of engagement. The intentions of the works move beyond verisimilitude into territories of evocation and experiential knowing. The realisation of the work as an experience in itself perhaps originates in a choice to express ideas poetically rather than via logical statements.

This choice to emphasise aesthetic experience can be understood as a move away from didacticism, yet it can still employ the kinds of rhetorical strategies that open conversation and provoke contemplation from audiences.

Rather than documenting an originating event, these films developed within a poetic approach become metaphorical representations that suggest ideas and experiences beyond the immediate range of the literal content that is used to represent the topic being explored. Shots and sequences may become more abstracted and expressionistic, so it is the experience of the work that becomes a way of knowing and thinking, rather than simply recognising the explicitly denoted content. Hans Georg Gadamer argues that:

> [i]n the experience of art we see a genuine experience induced by the work, which does not leave him who has it unchanged, and we enquire into the mode of being of that which is experienced in this way. So we hope to understand better what kind of truth it is that encounters us there. (cited in de Bolla 2002, 32)

Documentaries that are made according to a poetic approach embrace evocation as a guiding principle instead of acting as documents that provide factual proof or evidence. Freed from the requirements for objective representation and logical argument, the maker has licence to draw upon a fuller range of aesthetic tools than usually associated with attempts to appear balanced or neutral. Consequently, the sensory dimension of spectatorship is called upon, as memories are triggered through experiences that stimulate imagination and require an active, critical response. In a discussion of Marlon Riggs' *Tongues Untied* Renov points out that a strategy of evocation suggests that "the maker is less concerned with 'accurate' representation (a notion called into question by the powerful critiques of ethnography since the mid-1980s) and more with outlining the contours of experience, memory or sensation" (2007, 19). A key question is how Renov's description of evocation might apply to expanded media, and locative documentary in particular.

The rhetorical and compelling power of aesthetic experience for locative documentary lies in the way formal elements (which could include choice of location, system design, user interface, platform, and integration of wayfinding strategies) make it possible for an audience to bring their informal elements (such as experience, affect, memory, preconceptions, and subjectivity) to bear on and in the work. The aesthetic practice of combining these formal and informal elements enables connections that we can feel deeply as they occur within a contemplative space that uses poetic forms to focus deliberate attention and activate perceptual awareness. This is a poetic persuasion that is achieved by presence and absence. In the sharing of insights to experience and through the evocation of a shared sensory dimension, a communal space is established that emphasises presence in the here and now. An awareness of absence is created through deliberate gaps in representation, perhaps through low-resolution materials that inspire an affective yearning for the partial, imagined connection. In combination, these techniques can produce an aesthetic experience that allows for a moment of pause and different attention toward the material and durational experience of the work.

Therefore, the poetic work as an experience in itself choreographs combinations of images, sound, and concepts to thereby create heightened states that encourage the audience to look anew at things with which they are familiar and to spend time with things as yet unknown. For poetic documentary in particular (but perhaps also applicable to documentary more broadly), this can be a strategy that uses sensory input, memory recall, "hard" data, archival material, shared experience, and emotional responses to summon insight to the subjectivities and ideas being explored.

This kind of poetic strategy broadens our understanding of documentary, opening possibilities for documentary to be conceived of as an event, a conversation, a listening, an opportunity, a sharing, an environment, and a space of discussion. As Patricia Zimmermann points out, "a preliminary excavation into live multimedia performance has the potential to shift the ground of documentary history from the image to constructed, interactive environments and infiltration of different spaces that emphasise not individual artistry but collaboration" (293). These claims not only treat the ephemeral forms such as live audio-visual performance and participatory locative media as significant documentary practices in their own right, but also make evident the historical precedents for experience-based conceptions of documentary acts.

Utopic Dreams and Documentary Spaces

There is an almost utopic, optimistic and even, a reconciling impulse within the concept of *Finding Ways*. It is a socially engaged creative practice that continues the trajectory of my previous documentary work that explores techniques for individuals to connect with the perspectives of others, bridging differences in culture, values, and experience. I am seeking to encourage audience engagement with unfamiliar views of the world and personal histories by using aesthetic experience as a means for accessing additional layers of understanding. The intention is to use media arts practice to explore knowledge and experience beyond the horizons of the communities of which I am a part, and work to lessen fears about otherness and promote tolerance, possibly even change. In *Finding Ways* this exploration of difference and otherness is being taken up in the very form that the work is planned to take, that is, as sets of instructions.

Even in their directive mode, the instructions that *Finding Ways* relies upon open a space for interpretation, participation, and response. They work to establish a framework for experiencing location that urges participants to consider the broader contexts of their being in this place, now. Framing their quotidian experience through a range of intersecting and diverging perspectives, *Finding Ways* seeks to defamiliarise everyday spaces so that understandings and experiences that are beyond the individual or personal view are opened as potential fields for contemplation.

There can be a tendency in locative media for audience participants to become focused on the small screen of their mobile device, rather than on the interactions between location and media. Employing instructions as prompts that form the experience of the work is part of a method to explore ways to shift the focus from the device to the space that resonates *between* media and place. In using media in ways that allows for distracted, divided, and interrupted attention, the instructional form of *Finding Ways* refers the user outward, away from the screen, to the larger and more immersive canvas of the actual physical place. Even where supplemented by video and audio from source interview material, the primary layer of access in *Finding Ways* is through the instructional text. The focus is on an embodied experience of place that gains added depth through engaging with diverging perspectives from historical, political, industrial, and quotidian contexts as well as from the intersecting pathways of indigenous and migrant cultures. Participation in this work provides an opportunity to see and think through a different, alternative, and unfamiliar set of knowledges where the user's view of the place is shifted—their understanding and imagining of the instructor may be similarly impacted. The work will also prompt audience participants to contribute responses to the instructional text through social media and within a gallery installation that pulls data in from the project in the field. The intention is that these participant contributions will draw attention to gaps, oversights, and the contested perspectives that are likely to exist in the first, instruction-based layer of *Finding Ways*.

This combination of documentary practice and media delivered in specific locations with instructions about how to experience the place, and to which audience participants can respond, offers a strategy for negotiating complexity and "changefulness." As Ross Gibson has pointed out, activities such as documentary practice that "pledge an allegiance to the real world" (n.p.) need ways to explore its quickness, dynamism, and mutability. For example, in relation to indigenous understandings of place, it may be that connecting documentary practice to location can highlight a connection to country, issues of contestation of territory, and draw attention to conflicts around how place is enacted, and therefore understood, claimed, and managed. There is a need to consider how the multiplicity of place sits with notions of control and ownership of land and country. Does the virtual, in its very ephemerality, permit a way through these disputes? Just as place can hold multiple narratives, all existing simultaneously, the affordances of location-specific mobile media might allow multiple layers of information to be connected with the landscape. The locative may then present a mode of resistance to the physicality of borders and the fixity of other representational forms.

Zimmermann has written about the way documentary acts can create particular spaces as public domains "where ideas and exploring new vectors and relationships replace panic, amnesia and anaesthesia" (290). The idea that "new vectors and relationships" can "replace panic, amnesia and anaesthesia" is one that I find compelling and worthy of aspiration. This aspiration is a significant demand to place upon my media practice but could at the least provide alternatives to what Jon Dovey and Mandy Rose have critiqued as the "celebrations of one world-isms" (372) where representations of diversity tend to focus on social harmony, erasing conflict, and papering over differences that trouble.

This critique of practices that tends to ignore areas of unease and difference correspondingly emerges from Claire Bishop's proposal for a relational antagonism between art and all that might interfere with its realisation. In her incisive account of the relational aesthetic practices described by Nicolas Bourriaud, she points out that the kinds of microtopias produced by the predominantly installation works to which Bourriaud refers, are, just like utopia, "still predicated on the exclusion of those who hinder or prevent its realisation" (266). In place of art practices that rely upon social harmony for their foundation, Bishop proposes a concept of relational antagonism that would "provide more concrete and polemical grounds for rethinking our relationship to the world and to one another" (275).

Significantly for a documentary practice seeking to embrace the inherent changefulness of reality, both Zimmermann and Bishop's approaches acknowledge instability, complexity, and flux as the conditions of a democratic public sphere. Rather than pushing toward neat resolutions, each recognises the productive tension between the utopic dreams of an ideal society and the pragmatic necessity of understanding difference and change.

Finding Ways—II

> Choose a location with many intersecting pathways—footpaths, desire lines, histories, regulations, stakeholders, vested interests, inhabitants, visitors, tourists, passers-by, exiles, regulars, customers, merchants, officials, vagrants.
> Get to know this place deeply through spending time there over days and weeks.
> Haunt this place.
> If you can't actually take up residence, find other ways to let the location get under your skin.
> Research this place and make a list of who has a stake in the place, who spends time here, who makes money here, who has a history that connects them to this place, who has desires and longings that are embedded in this place.
> When you are feeling brave, seek out one of the people you have uncovered who you think might have a strong and unique vision of this place.
> Interview them and try to find out what things they believe are important about this place, what they notice, what they look for and what has shaped their perspectives.
> Ask them to select a specific spot that they feel strongly connected to.
> Translate the interview into a set of instructions for how to be in this chosen place. Resist any urges to soften the language or to smooth out rough edges. Instead, seek to be powerfully affected by the original content in order to approach a translation that evokes something of the original speaker's character.
> Repeat the process of talking [*and listening*] to people numerous times.
> Continue to translate the responses.
> Assume that there is an infinite number of ways that this place could be told.
> Realise that these tellings will always be incomplete.

Polyvocalities

Just as a democratic public sphere needs to embrace instability, complexity, and flux in order to remain democratic and public, so too our knowledges and understandings of place need to rely upon multiple voices to describe, with richness, the experiences that imbue a location with meaning. As Doreen Massey points out, places are not singular and fixed but are constantly coming into being through the way they are re-told, processed, and practiced. While some accounts will be officially sanctioned, it is important to retain the sense that there are many other ways to describe, explain, and interpret place. This density of description is key to any practice that seeks to reveal what might lie concealed behind appearances and to realise what remains unimagined due to our differing frames of reference and experience.

The strategy of *Finding Ways* then is to present place through multiple sets of instructions to participants on how to be there. With the elements presented as text-based instructions, they also hint at the underlying personal narratives that have shaped ways of perceiving and being in place. This is an approach that relies upon *polyvocalities*, "where more than one viewpoint is present and contradictions and disjunctures abound, opening up historical analysis to different explanatory models" (Zimmermann, 289). This also aligns with Bishop's ideas of relational antagonism and the value in keeping alive friction, awkwardness, and discomfort in order to expose "that which is repressed in sustaining the semblance of… harmony" (275).

The polyvocal strategy of *Finding Ways* provides significant scope to explore antagonisms resulting from the disparities between varying and differing perspectives that are presented and then accessed through the instructional texts. The application of a flat nodal structure to content in *Finding Ways* lessens the sense of hierarchical organisation and goes some way to decentre what might otherwise be viewed as privileged or officially sanctioned perspectives. Each set of instructions will be tied to a specific locale and the movement of the audience participant through the location will determine the order of encounter. The affordances of HTML code, such as hyperlinking and tagging, also provide the opportunity to highlight overlaps between the content of the instructions. For example, a system of horizontal linking that draws on keyword tagging could make connections between spatial, emotional, sensory, and other thematic references, and also draw attention to the ways that the instructions diverge in their responses to common stimuli.

In addition to the divergent viewpoints conveyed through the instructional texts there is the opportunity for further relational antagonism to develop as the audience participants encounter the instructed activities that are integral to the process of experiencing the documentary. The quality of the relationships and exchanges enabled by the project that arise between instructions, responses, and audience participants are significant in determining the nature of the aesthetic encounters that are experienced. In fact, these relational spaces may be viewed as the true or essential aesthetic material of the *Finding Ways* project.

Documentary as Instructions/Instructions as Documentary

Anna Dezeuze describes instruction-based art as "a practice that exists only through a potential participation" (3–4). Consequently, the role that audience participants are permitted to play in the construction and life of the work is concurrently an ethical and an aesthetic choice with the power to produce a range of potential experiences. For instance, in the work of the Fluxus artists, who are identified as strong proponents of an instruction-based approach to art, there are a variety of modes employed for audience involvement, extending from emancipatory and open to constrained and closed. For example, Karen O'Rourke has observed that "[u]nlike Cage, who encouraged audience participation as a way of relinquishing 'authorial control,' Kaprow used audience members as 'props through which the artist's vision was executed'" (75). Hence the manner in which audience participants are invited and given opportunities to participate in *Finding Ways* will affect the nature of the interaction between the work, audience participants, and place, and the kind of public domains that may be created. In exploring alternate forms for documentary practice, a major motivation in *Finding Ways* is to disrupt the didacticism that can often be associated with documentary. The disruptive impulse that an instructional approach offers has the potential to impact broadly across a range of rhetorical techniques that are used in expanded forms of documentary.

Participatory Documentary

There is a multilayered rationale for the participative aspects of the *Finding Ways* project. Audience responses and contributions that are incorporated into *Finding Ways* continue the contextualising of place that is commenced in the instruction texts. This new material provides the means to maintain a quickness of experience and delays fixity of form or understanding. The opening of the work to public contributions allows the piece to evolve and develop over time as people engage with and respond to the instructions. The audience responses to the instruction texts in *Finding Ways* will form an important part of the overall documentary act, enabling polyvocality and the sort of relational antagonism that Bishop (2012) advocates. Not only will this contributed material constitute a complex archive of responses to the text, but in the processing, tagging, and interrogation of the material, gaps, and ruptures may be exposed that may otherwise go unrecognised.

The instruction texts within *Finding Ways* will focus on the everyday. My goal is to produce the instructions as poetic texts that mix stylistic approaches including being challenging, confronting, entertaining, beautiful, lyrical, enchanting, rigorous, musical, funny, wry, witty, sad, reflexive, avant-garde, earthy, matter-of-fact, bare, baroque, seductive, and charming. This poetic strategy is intended to shift modes of perception and prompt a different type of attention to place. Within an expanded field of documentary practice there is an intrinsic value available in the experience of the work, as it requires enacting. Through the way the work is performed the audience can be guided to slow down and focus, even momentarily, on a particular set of qualities that may have otherwise passed them by.

While instructions can be perceived as procedural texts it does not have to follow that the activities described in the instructions of *Finding Ways* are achievable or will be obeyed. By their nature, instructions set out a course of actions that proceed in a step-by-step manner, most often with a particular result to be achieved. However, resistant, contrarian, and indifferent interpretations are valid responses that demonstrate evidence of audience agency in relation to the instructions, and can become part of the project's relational antagonism. There may be contemplative benefits in instructions that pose conundrums for participants to turn over and play with in their mind. In addition, the inclusion of instructions that are impossible to perform brings the authority and trustworthiness of the particular instructor (and potentially all the other instructions) playfully into question. A new perspective may arise in the pauses created by the shock of an impossible process or a puzzle that requires consideration and thereby slows thought down.

Provocation and Shift

The notion of creating instructions by distilling material drawn from interviews takes its cue from the collaborations between film-maker Brian Hill and poet Simon Armitage on documentary projects such as "Drinking for England" (1998) and "Feltham Sings" (2005). In these works, which have been described by Paget and Roscoe as "documentary musical (or documusical)," interviews were conducted and then reworked into "*purpose-composed* verse, music and song" (Paget and Roscoe, n.p.) to be performed by the original interviewees. As they observe,

> An especially provocative shift in spectator-position occurs at the moments when participants in documentary musical shift from documentary interviewee to musical performer. At such production nodes we are suddenly cut free from a conventional point-of-audition/point-of-view and aligned in an altogether new way with the documentary subject. (n.p.)

It is this kind of "provocative shift" that I am attempting to achieve with the interview-derived instruction texts in *Finding Ways.* These instructions are not aiming to reproduce experiences and situations but to shape another space by offering alternative ways to think, imagine, and to experience place.

For example, Megan Heyward's locative artwork, *Notes for Walking* (2013) consisted of thirteen video notes that aimed to change the quality of participants' attention to specific locations on Middle Head, in Sydney. Arising out of Heyward's research into spatial narrative, walked practices, and the augmented landscapes produced by earlier cultural practices such as pilgrimages (Heyward 2014), this work used the Japanese form of the *go-eika*, a set of poetic texts that direct pilgrims on the island of Shikoku to consider the physical setting through which they are walking. The notes in Heyward's work function like a set of instructions shaping ways of perceiving and experiencing the landscape. While not strictly a work of documentary, *Notes for Walking* is nonetheless relevant for the ways in which poetic fragments are connected to a specific location in highly evocative ways.

In some respects, *Finding Ways* can be considered a literary exercise. The placement of the instructions within the landscape is akin to a practice of reading in place, and while the plan is to include material from the source interviews this is conceived of as supplemental to the instructions, rather than the focus of the work. The link to documentary practice is in the experiences that the instructions prompt, the thinking that informs the instructions, and in the subjective insights that the instructions might enable. It is then a speculative form of documentary in how it relies upon the audience participant's imaginative engagement with the restrictions, which as Brogan Bunt has observed, is enacted in "the interplay between general definition and specific realisation" (11).

Finding Ways—III

> Now it's time to seed the instructions in the landscape and prepare the way for others to contribute to the project.
> You'll need
>
> - Your completed instructions
> - A way for people to find and access the instructions on location
> - A way for people to tag and respond to the instructions
> - A way for people to access the content that other participants contribute.
>
> Sounds easy, doesn't it?
> Oh, but hang on. If you want to do this participation thing properly it can't just be an add-on. All the thought, effort and care that went into preparing the instructions need to be matched, if not exceeded by the effort and care you put into designing and realising this part of the project.
> So, you'll need to: find ways to motivate people to participate; design an interface that is appealing and relevant to the content; include directions of how to do the work and help people to find their way; develop a location-aware web app; debug the code; consider the privacy issues in getting participants to allow you access to their location; manage the contributions people make; worry about issues of participant safety on location; maybe provide wireless internet to improve participant access to content; troubleshoot the different combinations of mobile device, browser, service provider, and user literacy that could stop the whole thing from working…
> I could go on.
>
> There's a lot more to think about.
>
> Do you wish to continue?

Documentary as Locative Media/Locative Media as Documentary

One consequence of realising the *Finding Ways* project through a spatialised walking practice is that it permits a rethinking and perhaps expansion of how we understand the form of documentary. Sited in the imbricated space of an augmented reality where media is set up to resonate with location, walking acts as one interface for the interactive, location-specific documentary and permits a shifting engagement with place. For participants, the walk they take, shaped by the *Finding Ways* content and instruction-based prompts, becomes a literal journey through the multiple layers that constitute the place of its execution. An experience of the complex imaginings possible in the overlap of the stories that make up the layers of place is actualised through this physical, real world meander. As an aesthetic experience, details are brought into focus to permit an engagement with a changeful and shifting reality. The different ways that we can then experience place—physically, sensorially, emotionally, socially, politically, historically, economically, imaginatively, culturally—highlight the diverse ways of knowing that this documentary project is calling upon. Explorations within *Finding Ways* can then follow these non-linear paths of knowing, made up of memory and thematic interconnections as the location is navigated via virtual points of interest.

Finding Ways will anchor content to geographic coordinates via mobile, networked systems and facilitate the annotation of this locative media. The intention is to explore the complexities of place and to manifest the divergent narratives that reside within it. Like a palimpsest, our understandings of place are dense and multilayered, overwritten with inscriptions from history, institutional discourse, social utility, individual memory, physical characteristics, environmental context, weather, politics, economics, emotion—and that's to name but a few of the possible strata.

However, for this aggregate of information to be a documentary act some degree of further processing needs to happen. As Philip Rosen argues, it is through the synthesising and sequencing of documents that acts of documentary occur. In Rosen's formulation the documentarian's task is to transform unprocessed data or information into meaningful, knowledgeable and rhetorical works, thereby becoming a "synthesizer of reality against the unmediated, unorganized index" (89). This is a process of translating data (including perceptual input) into knowledge through the ordering and contextualisation of raw material. Rosen's concept shows that documentary makers have always played a curatorial role in presenting a diverse range of content. However, the participatory aspects of *Finding Ways* have the potential to take documentary beyond the curatorial control of an auteur as the work loses its authorial focus and has the capacity to take on an emergent life of its own.

The synthesising that occurs within locative participatory projects includes aesthetic and procedural decisions that shape user experience as well as the selection and presentation of more traditional documentary material including archival footage, interviews and data visualisation. When working with interactive, participatory, and collaborative forms of interactive documentary it is fundamental to enable active modes of audience engagement through the project's interaction design, particularly in the face of what Jeff Ritchie has termed the requirement of "really non-trivial effort" (57) to navigate and understand mobile locative narrative. He notes that the story space of these kinds of projects:

> has the possibility of being harder to understand, due to its existing across two different media spaces to be explored, being potentially bigger than other types of narratives, and requiring audiences to constantly discern what does or doesn't belong within the storyworld. (Ritchie, 57–58)

Ritchie goes on to conclude that "[t]o more readily afford these interactions, mobile locative narratives must provide audiences with wayfinding information and narrative bridges" (65) that somehow connect the virtual and real-world materials.

The instructions that are fundamental to *Finding Ways* provide a way to integrate narrative wayfinding as a core part of the project's aesthetic. Consequently, there is scope to accommodate the documentary acts of synthesis and sequencing through these instructions while also assisting audience participants to navigate and make sense of the media that they encounter.

In a 2006 article that provided a survey of the development of locative media, Marc Tuters and Kazys Varnelis highlighted that:

> Since its inception, then, locative media's practitioners have claimed an avant-garde position, insisting not only that their work is capable of creating a paradigmatic shift in the art world, but also that it can reconfigure our everyday life as well by renewing our sense of place in the world (358).

Eleven years later the avant-garde position described by Tuters and Varnelis is now the terrain of marketers and advertisers that target customers with location-aware messages frequently informed by patterns of consumption and movement mined from the histories of browsers and smartphone location services. While the locative is new terrain for documentary practice, there is a well-developed infrastructure of developers, platforms, applications, and devices for the creation and delivery of locative content. For expanded documentary practices, it becomes a matter of repurposing these technologies within a remit for what Zimmermann has described as "engaging colligation to generate epistemological questioning" (297).

Enmeshed in Media—Documentary Acts, Relations, and Experiences

This chapter was written to explore the impact that emerging technological forms have on the way we conceive of documentary acts. I have argued that if we consider documentary from the point of view of an aesthetic experience with particular, documentary rhetorical intentions, then we may be better placed to take advantage of new media forms, systems, and technologies within an expanded understanding of documentary practice.

The possibility of realising an instruction-based documentary artwork that is mobile, site-specific, and screen-based has been used as a hypothetical example. Locative media has the potential to expand the field of documentary rhetoric because it is able to emphasise the embodied experience of digital content as it resonates between the user and the real-world point of access. Complementing this, the use of poetic language to render an artistic approach to the procedural instruction texts of the *Finding Ways* project can direct attention to the physical world, in situ, and offer alternative ways for perceiving the immediate environment.

This is an approach and method for site-specific, instruction-based artwork that utilises the key documentary making skills of researching and interviewing before developing audio-visual strategies to convey concepts and to sequence the material into meaningful patterns. The objective of this method is to guide the documentary audience participant through a series of directed experiences as a way to provoke situated knowledges about place that arise from sensory engagement, and to give the opportunity to consider other perspectives.

Bibliography

Bishop, Claire. "Antagonism and Relational Aesthetics." *The 'Do-It-Yourself' Artwork: Participation from Fluxus to New Media*. Ed. Anna Dezeuze. Manchester: Manchester University Press, 2012. 257–280.

Bunt, Brogan. "Instructions." *Brogan Bunt*, April 30, 2011, Web.

De Bolla, Peter. "Toward the Materiality of Aesthetic Experience." *Diacritics* 32.1 (2002): 19–37.

Dezeuze, Anna. "An Introduction to the 'Do-It-Yourself' Artwork." *The 'Do-It-Yourself' Artwork: Participation from Fluxus to New Media*. Ed. Anna Dezeuze. Manchester: Manchester University Press, 2012. 1–21.

Dovey, Jon, and Mandy Rose. "'This Great Mapping of Ourselves': New Documentary Forms Online." *The Documentary Film Book*. Ed. Brian Winston. London: Palgrave Macmillan, 2013. 366–375.

Gibson, Ross. "The Creative Pursuit of Everchanging Actuality." Paper Presented at *Expanded Documentary Seminar – Event/Document/Documentary*, Faculty of Creative Arts, University of Wollongong, September 6, 2012.

Grierson, John, and Forsyth Hardy. *Grierson on Documentary*. Abridged ed. London: Faber, 1979.

Heyward, Megan. *Notes for Walking*. Artwork, Mosman Art Gallery, Sydney, 2013.

Heyward, Megan. *Notes for Walking an Augmented Landscape: Spatial Narrative, Walking Practices and Locative Technologies*. DCA thesis. Sydney: University of Technology Sydney, 2014.

Hill, Brian (dir.), and Simon Armitage (writer). *Drinking for England*. Century Films, United Kingdom, 1998.

Hill, Brian (dir.), Roger Graef (prod.), and Simon Armitage (writer). *Feltham Sings*. ABC, Sydney, New South Wales, 2005.

Massey, Doreen B. *For Space*. London: SAGE, 2008.

Nichols, Bill. *Introduction to Documentary*. 2nd ed. Bloomington: Indiana University Press, 2010.

O'Rourke, Karen. *Walking and Mapping: Artists as Cartographers*. London: The MIT Press, 2013.

Paget, Derek, and Jane Roscoe. "Giving Voice: Performance and Authenticity in the Documentary Musical", *Jump Cut* 48, 2006, Web.

Renov, Michael. "Towards a Poetics of Documentary." *Theorizing Documentary*. Ed. Michael Renov. New York: Routledge, 1993. 12–36.

Renov, Michael. *The Subject of Documentary: Visible Evidence*. Minneapolis: University of Minnesota Press, 2004.

Renov, Michael. "Away from Copying: The Art of Documentary Practice." *Truth or Dare: Art & Documentary*. Ed. Gail Pearce and Cahal McLaughlin. Bristol: Intellect, 2007. 13–24.

Ritchie, Jeff. "The Affordances and Constraints of Mobile Locative Narratives." *The Mobile Story: Narrative Practices with Locative Technologies*. Ed. Jason Farman. New York: Routledge, 2013. 53–67.

Rosen, Philip. "Document and Documentary: On the Persistence of Historical Concepts." *Theorizing Documentary*. Ed. Michael Renov. New York: Routledge, 1993. 58–89.

Tuters, Marc, and Kazys Varnelis. "Beyond Locative Media: Giving Shape to the Internet of Things." *Leonardo* 39.4 (2006): 357–363.

Zimmermann, Patricia R. "Public Domains: Engaging Iraq Through Experimental Documentary Digitalities." *Rethinking Documentary: New Perspectives, New Practices*. Ed. Wilma de Jong and Thomas Austin. Buckingham: Open University, 2008. 284–298.

The Documentary Designer: A List of Propositions for Interactive Documentary Practice Online

Seth Keen

Abstract This chapter proposes that interactive documentary needs to utilise the affordances of the network in a way similar to other online media. To help with this, documentary can use design methods to identify the affordances of the network to then connect media into a web of relations. Design in this context is also a process that responds to problems that arise through change, and this ability to negotiate change is key in the fast-paced environment of the Internet.

Keywords Interactive documentary • Documentary • Design • User experience design • Interaction design • Design and documentary

In this chapter I propose that for interactive documentary to progress it needs to adopt design methodologies that help utilise the affordances of the network, in a similar manner to other successful online media. To do this, interactive documentary must find ways to integrate design practices

---

S. Keen (✉)
School of Media and Communication, RMIT University,
Melbourne, VIC, Australia

A. Miles (ed.), *Digital Media and Documentary*,
https://doi.org/10.1007/978-3-319-68643-1_4

into media making. Many online media platforms have taken advantage of the affordances of the network to connect information, media, and people into a web of relations, and these platforms have relied upon design practices to inform their development as social media tools and services. Design in this context can be considered as a process that responds to problems that arise through change, and this is why design has become a key feature of many of the practices associated with the fast-paced development of the Internet. For interactive documentary to adapt to the constant transformations occurring in online media it is design's ability to negotiate change in the context of applied outcomes that provides important methods for interactive documentary.

Documentary Design

Design methodologies as an integral aspect of interactive documentary practice is not an entirely new concept. Theorists like O'Flynn (2012), and Dovey and Rose (2012), have written of documentary design. O'Flynn, for example, evaluates the emergence of different forms of interactive documentary across multiple platforms and connects these developments with the incorporation of design methods into documentary practice. O'Flynn proposes that:

> notions of interactivity have changed over the past decade … [due to] a shift away from a binaristic "choose your own adventure" orientation towards plot as an either/or structure and narrative causality to an exploration of experiential interface design. Here, i-docs of the last five years have demonstrated an increasing attention to interface and user experience design as dynamic structural elements expressive of a thematic core to the given narrative. (2012, 156)

In joining O'Flynn, my focus is on design as a key component of interactive documentary practice. This also involves the use of a practice-led methodology in my research to find out what it is to enact design methodologies in an interactive documentary practice.

The Documentary Designer

Documentary practice is transformed in the multilinear architecture of the Internet, requiring a reconceptualisation of the term "documentary maker." A practitioner who makes interactive documentary on the Internet is now more accurately described as a "documentary designer." In support of this role, I am proposing a list of terms or concepts that a documentary designer is required to understand.

This notion of a documentary designer emerges from my position as a practitioner and the projects, tools, and approaches to interactive documentary practice tested through academic and industry research. I have produced artefacts that offer propositions about documentary design, and what it means to be a documentary designer. This practice-led approach has opened up possibilities for me to rethink interactive documentary through the concept of documentary design as a new mode of practice that future makers will be required to understand.

I define the role of a documentary designer, and the practices they enact, through the broad categories of interactive media, affordance, web of relations, and design methodology. I introduce what these categories are, and then use these categories, combined with the notion of dexterity, to list the key propositions that underwrite what I believe a documentary designer needs to know and do.

Categories

Interactive Media

Interactive documentaries are situated within interactive digital media more broadly, and interactivity is a distinguishing feature of these forms. Gaudenzi (2013) argues that in an interactive documentary the audience must be able to tangibly make something happen in or to the work, while Ryan (2004) suggests that interactivity involves more than just publishing media online. As an example Ryan proposes that the online publication of a movie, as it was produced for cinema, does not alter in any way how the work is presented to the audience. Interactivity changes media's "ability to tell stories, and the stories it can tell" (Ryan 2004, 338), and if a cinematic or televisual documentary published on the Internet is not yet interactive we can see that an interactive documentary requires its topic to be presented in a different way. For example, the documentary *Planet Galata* (2010) was produced for television and as an interactive documentary. In the interactive version, made using Thalhofer's Korsakow software, video is fragmented into independent granules that can be viewed in varying orders. In their own description of their television version, Bas and Thalhofer claim that it "is exactly the same every time you look at it. Every scene is glued to each other once and forever." However, in their interactive documentary the topic is presented differently to the television version because of its varying pathways and ordering. Thalhofer proposes that because a Korsakow film creates multiple pathways it is a more fluid experience for the user (Crossover Labs 2015).

Affordances

In the *Design of Everyday Things* Norman defines affordance as the "perceived and actual properties of the thing, primarily those fundamental properties that determine how the thing could possibly be used" (1998, 9). Each individual medium in an interactive documentary has particular affordances that need to be identified to inform interactive documentary practice online. What will matter to interactive documentary are the particularly affordances that arise from video, computers, and the network, and these affordances are granularity, remix, indexing, and spatial montage.

Granularity is an affordance of video and in interactive documentary it is how "granules" of video are able to remain independent in computers and on the network. With shots or sequences separate there is the option to create multiple relations between them, which alters the way a work can be structured to convey meaning. With this granularity the computer then enables the affordances of remix, indexing, and spatial montage for interactive documentary. Remix refers to the computer's ability to combine and recombine video, including the audience's ability to mix media on the computer including appropriating it for other purposes. Remix is an important consideration in interaction design as it forms an integral part of the user engaging with the work. Indexing refers to the use of metadata to allow for the access and retrieval of stored content on a computer. In an interactive documentary indexing is used to form relations between granules and create an overarching structure that ties the work together as a whole. Spatial montage describes the ability to have multiple windows open concurrently on a computer, as argued by Manovich (2001). In the design of the interface for an interactive documentary working with video both temporally and spatially is involved. Finally, network is defined as the infrastructure of computers that make up the World Wide Web, consisting of a series of protocols and servers that run on the Internet that facilitates the four affordances of granularity, remix, indexing, and spatial montage.

Web of Relations

The World Wide Web as a network has a multilinear structure that enables a web of relations to be created between multiple granules of video in an interactive documentary. These videos can be then remixed into different combinations. As a concept, "web of relations" describes how associations are formed between this content in the multilinear structure provided by the World Wide Web. I use Bordwell and Thompson's (2010) definition of "nonnarrative" to describe the particular form of interactive documentary I am discussing. In regards to the form of a documentary in a linear structure Bordwell and Thompson focus on how relations are organised between shots in a "narrative" and "nonnarrative" manner. In a narrative a linear structure is utilised to convey one situation leading to another as part of an ongoing "cause and effect" framework. Bordwell and Thompson propose that to create relations between shots in a non-narrative film material is arranged using a taxonomy and that this provides a structured process of classification, in effect creating a linear web of relations. Following Bordwell and Thompson, documentary can be classified into four modes of linear narrative, linear non-narrative, multilinear narrative, and multilinear non-narrative. In the case of interactive documentary, it is multilinear non-narrative that best exemplifies the affordances and web of relations that I am discussing.

Design as Methodology

Design methodology refers to the designerly processes that need to be integrated into the production of an interactive documentary. It is these design methodologies that allow the documentary designer to negotiate the intersection of documentary and new media. Design thinking is often described as a process that involves reframing a problem to understand and define it (Buchanan 1992, Kimbell 2011). Designers are problem-orientated practitioners who integrate hands-on skills with conceptual ideas, thinking through their making to create solutions to problems.

Design thinking recognises that artefacts are propositions that are ideas. As Kimbell, discussing Buchanan's seminal 1992 "Wicked Problems in Design Thinking" notes, design thinking "could be applied to nearly anything, whether a tangible object or intangible system," and that design is "well-placed to serve the needs of a technological culture in which many kinds of things are designed, and human problems are complex"

(2011, 292). Kimbell goes on to suggest that "the designer brings a unique way of looking at problems and finding solutions" (292). Design thinking methodologies are able to be used in an agile way to engage with the problems, and determine the strategies and practices required, to work in an environment that is undergoing rapid transformation such as we see with interactive documentary and the World Wide Web.

The Propositions

Using these categories of interactive media, affordance, web of relations, and design methodology I propose the following propositions for documentary design.

Taken together the following propositions provide a starting point that describes the documentary designer as an emerging role in the documentary project in relation to interactive documentary.

1. The documentary designer designs and produces interactive media across a range of platforms in a variety of contexts.

Nash refers to the evolving and experimental development of documentary form, and recognises the formation of interactive documentaries on multiple platforms. She writes:

> As new media technologies and new forms of communication emerge, contemporary documentary makers are engaging in a process of actively rethinking the documentary project. They are imagining what documentary might become: non-linear, multimedia, interactive, hybrid, cross-platform, convergent, virtual, or something else as yet un-thought. Within this experimental space the webdoc has become an established mode of documentary production. (2012, 197)

Similarily, O'Flynn (2012) acknowledges a transformation in documentary practice and the rapidly evolving nature of interactive documentary. As a consequence practitioners engaging with interactive documentaries are producing works outside of traditional film and television models, and developing new frameworks for this engagement is necessary for working with new technologies and platforms.

2. The documentary designer makes content for "lean-forward" users.

In an examination of the difference between television and the web, Nielsen (2008) uses the terms "lean-back" and "lean-forward" to differentiate between the two mediums. Television is described as a "passive medium" that is lean-back, whereas the Web is an "active medium" that is lean-forward. Interactivity in television is limited to changing channels, while DVD players and video-on-demand only offer options to rewind, forward, and pause. However, these actions are tied solely to the activity of viewing and do not alter the structure of what is being viewed. A web user on the other hand expects to have some type of engagement in the formation of a work. Nielsen's differentiation between lean-back and lean-forward represents a change in the role of the audience where the audience for television and cinema documentaries are "lean-back," while interactive documentary audiences are "lean-forward" participants involved in the construction of the work. In an interactive documentary a user is expected to do more than simply turn a computer on and view clips for playback, instead they navigate their way through a database, assembling a work from the content available within a particular system.

3. The documentary designer has strategies to work with the ephemeral nature of what is designed and produced.

Merrin (2010) claims that digital media is ephemeral because of the tenuous state of hardware and software, and the momentary production and consumption of content. In an evaluation of producing interactive documentaries online, Matt Soar, one of the developers of the interactive video software Korsakow, states:

> Choosing a software platform for any kind of project is, as much as anything else, an exercise in playing the odds: quite apart from cost, reliability, documentation and support. What if one or more factors (the programming language, the platform, the operating system, the plugins, the versioning) prove to be relatively short-lived? (2014, 157)

As Soar argues, it is highly likely that many interactive documentaries made now will not be available for viewing in the future due to software updates and the works not being preserved in a way that allows them to be archived for viewing. Code, codecs, applications, and standards are constantly changing, so this is a field defined by impermanence and change.

4. The documentary designer understands that tools are not permanent and fixed, are a means to an end, and that they constantly change and are superseded.

The tools for making interactive documentaries are constantly evolving, with new programs and platforms appearing while old ones decline. Like all software they require constant updates to meet the requirements of changing technologies, which promotes changing practices. The ongoing development of Korsakow provides an example of the evolving state of interactive video software. On the Korsakow "Release Notes" web page, improvements and fixes to versions of the software are documented (Soar and Thalhofer 2005). These changes reflect what is required to work with Korsakow, with alterations occurring across HTML web standards, programming languages, plug-ins, browsers, video players, and operating systems, along with the ongoing modifications to the program itself. If tools are not constantly updated, other tools supersede them, and due to the way in which tools function, this causes a shift in practice. For instance, a community of practitioners currently shares technical and production knowledge that has been built up around Korsakow, if Korsakow becomes obsolete, this community of practitioners will move to other programs or platforms and this can be expected to bring new approaches towards practice.

5. The documentary designer accepts that new technologies and practices will have to be created, and this involves being open to working with software, hardware, and practices from other fields.

The notion of repurposing software for other uses and practices points towards interactive documentary practitioners being prepared to innovate to see how existing software can be used to meet their own aims. This process of reusing existing software has a connection with Manovich's (2008) concept of media production on the web being informed by a "tactical model"; a form of production that facilitates flexibility, with the ability to access code and rewrite it for other purposes.

6. The documentary designer requires knowledge of code to work with interaction designers and programmers.

Interactive documentary can be created in custom-built systems or by using existing off-the-shelf programs and Content Management

Systems (CMS). Custom-built systems require development and the nurturing of a project team that needs to include developers and interaction designers. A project like *Prison Valley* (2010) is an example of a project that relied on the bespoke development of a web project that was programmed and designed. Another option is to use off-the-shelf tools such as Korsakow or Klynt. These programs provide a relatively cost effective option to create interactive documentaries without the resourcing often required for building individual platforms or sites. While many of these off-the-shelf tools are designed to be user friendly, in most cases some understanding of code is valuable to allow customisation and creative development of the interactive documentaries made. In addition, when developing an interactive documentary that does not rely on existing authoring programs or platforms, a comprehension of code is needed for the documentary designer to understand and communicate what is to be designed, and why, to the development team in relation to interaction design and user experience.

7. The documentary designer understands the affordances of the formats they are working with in relation to content, the interaction of the user, and the digital platforms that are used.

According to Norman (1999) a person brings to an object prior knowledge, and has particular goals, in regard to the relationship they have with an object. In turn, an object can do some things and not others, that is, it has affordances. Good design, for Norman, is to make these affordances apparent and obvious for the user. However, in some cases, preconceived knowledge or experience can lead towards outcomes that are not utilising the affordances of the mediums being used. For instance, documentary practitioners who have predominately produced linear narrative often aim to do the same in interactive media. As Miles in "Softvideography: Digital Video as Postliterate Practice" argues:

> Desktop tools have largely concentrated on maintaining "film and video" as hegemonic aesthetic material objects ... as a linear, time-based object that consists principally of a sound and image track. (2008a, 10)

Miles draws attention here to how producers have not acknowledged the affordances of the mediums used and have remained wedded to traditional forms.

8. The documentary designer has the ability to determine which affordances matter, and how these affordances will be made available.

Norman (1998) argues that interaction designers need to concentrate on turning the abstract qualities of a computer into perceivable and comprehensible affordances that can be used easily like any other everyday thing. Therefore, a major consideration for the documentary designer is indicating to the audience how to engage with an interactive documentary, with the challenge being to design interfaces that make the affordances of the work perceivable and integrated in a usable manner.

9. The documentary designer understands granularity as an affordance where fragments of content are independent, and offering meaning in a self-sufficient way. They are conscious of how the degree of granularity affects the complexity of the system of relations that is created.

In making a documentary shots are recorded then edited together on a timeline to make a linear work. The completed documentary is one video file made up of numerous shots. In contrast, computers and the network provide the option to present video as separate files, what Manovich in *The Language of New Media* (2001) describes as "modularity." For Manovich, modularity is the notion that digital media is made up of independent parts that can be divided into smaller units that can remain separate. Modularity then describes granularity, and granularity, as Miles explains:

> Granularity is a term that is appropriated from hypertext and refers to the smallest meaningful unit within a system. In hypertext this would be a node, in a blog it would probably be a post, and in video this is the shot. Obviously what constitutes "smallest" and "meaningful" are sensitive to different contexts, so that in classical hypertext a node could contain a single word, a phrase, or several paragraphs, as could a blog post, and of course a shot could be of extremely brief duration through to the recent examples of 90 minute plus continuous takes. (2008b, 223)

The ability to keep video as separate granules represents a significant change for documentary makers in regards to how relations between shots are structured. As Brooks suggests "by using smaller story granules, there are more ways in which they can fit together" (1996, 327). Now the documentary designer is faced with multiple relations between shots, and determining the scale of granularity, and subsequently the level of complexity of the work is a key decision.

10. The documentary designer is aware that the computational attributes of a computer can be used to facilitate the creation of work that is no longer static and fixed. Such remix allows the user to create varying combinations from content.

Interactive documentary has the potential to use computational procedures to facilitate the creation of generative work. For example, when video is kept as separate files that can be remixed then an interactive documentary is not fixed like a film and television documentary. Murray describes these processes as a "procedural affordance," where a computer has the "ability to represent and execute conditional behaviours" (2012, 51). These procedural properties allow video files to be organised into different combinations. A connection can be made here with Douglas' analysis of remix in hypertext:

> Until a reader assembles it, performing it, the text exists only as a set of potential motions, a sequence of steps and maneuvers that become actualised only the instant that the reader selects a segment of text and fulfills a condition for movement. (1999, 31)

As a result, interactive documentaries are always variable and different users might experience different works.

11. The documentary designer is able to use "indexing" to form multiple relations between shots.

In the Web 2.0 phase of the Internet indexing, via informal tagging, is a widely used method to curate content. This indexing takes advantage of what Murray (2012) has described as the computer's "encyclopedic affordance" that utilises the potential to store large volumes of information in varying types of collections. Indexing allows an interactive documentary to classify video for access and retrieval. For example, the interactive documentary *Gaza Sderot* (2008) provides an unordered list that allows users to access content based on tags. Here indexing allows separate shots and sequences to be grouped into different collections and so these shots and sequences are able to function independently within a larger whole. The documentary designer therefore needs to consider the role of indexing to structure interactive documentaries.

12. The documentary designer knows that spatiality is as important as temporality, and that spatial montage as an affordance provides opportunities to collage shots together in space and time.

Manovich (2001) proposes that spatial montage is the manipulation of the screen as a fluid, multi-windowed interface. The spatial composition of multiple windows in the screen is due to what Murray describes as "virtual space" (2012, 70). On a computer, and in the network, independent shots held in a directory or database can be called into windows within the screen using programming and action scripts. The composition of multiple windows can also change. In Korsakow, for example, each video clip can be assigned to a different interface and multiple window compositions designed. Virtual space provides the producer with different ways to collage shots, both temporally and spatially, compared to fixed split-screen compositions in cinema and television. Dovey and Rose, using Mozilla's *Popcorn Maker* to demonstrate their case, argue that tools like these give a "foretaste of how spatial montage that includes types of web data can become a vernacular, a 'camera stylo' for web documentary" (2012, 14). This vernacular is yet to be developed.

Web of Relations

13. In a work with no set duration the documentary designer learns how to include, rather than exclude, material on a topic.

When shooting and then editing film and television documentary it is common for there to be a very high ratio between what is filmed and what ends up in the final edit. Editing then involves selecting a small amount of shots from the available material and discarding the rest. For a traditional linear edit the aim is to work out what to discard. In contrast, in interactive documentary it is possible to make open works of no set duration, therefore the documentary designer is not restricted in the amount of video material that can be retained. In an interactive documentary that has no set duration there is then the potential to include material that would otherwise be discarded in a linear documentary. This then raises questions for the documentary designer of how to structure and allow access to potentially hundreds of hours of video. This is where granularity and indexing become significant as ways to allow discoverable connections between videos in interactive documentary. This is in contrast to shots being constrained in a sequential linear work to relations with the shot before and after on the timeline, within a set duration of time. The ability to retain what has been filmed, in combination with the capacity to form a web of relations between shots, enables the complexities of a topic to be conveyed, and an unlimited number of perspectives included.

14. The documentary designer can work within structures that may have no beginning, middle, or end.

Where an interactive documentary employs a multilinear structure there is the possibility to create multilinear works with no beginning, middle, or end. When a work no longer has a definite ending and is multilinear, then sequences are formed through the work by following trails from one part to another. These parts create a whole through the associations created between them. The documentary designer working with this form of documentary needs to create sequences that are able to exist independently of each other, yet also support associative relations that let these parts connect together in multiple ways.

15. The documentary designer understands that work may not be viewed in its entirety, and may have multiple viewings.

When an interactive documentary has no beginning, middle, or end users enter the work at different points, choose to view some material, then leave. Each user may then have a different experience depending on where they enter the work and how long they stay. Repetition then becomes an expected norm as some viewers will return to the same content several times. This presents challenges to practitioners who are used to linear work for the documentary designer has to consider these new viewing conditions.

16. The documentary designer is able to refer to other structures, for example taxonomic schemas, rather than the narratives that have historically been created in linear documentary.

Exploring new forms of documentary that do not rely on the linear hegemony of a start and end point has the potential to refer to other structures, for example taxonomic schemas, rather than the narratives that have historically been created in linear documentary. This risks the formlessness of a "pure open structure" (Plantinga 1997, 135), what Ryan (2004), in the broader example of interactive media, proposes is a risk when the web of relations becomes too random. Shifting to a structure like a taxonomic schema lessens these risks and is driven by the remix affordances of computers and the network, and the fluid, changing potential of interactive documentary as a work. Having the ability to refer to other structures outside traditional documentary practice for television and cinema enables the documentary designer to utilise affordances like indexing and remix more effectively to portray a topic.

Design Methodologies

17. The documentary designer works iteratively as a reflective practitioner (Schön 1983) to reflect on what is made and use this reflection to inform what is made next.

Design as a practice generally starts with a process of making and using the outcomes of this making in a cyclic manner to inform decisions. In design the practitioner is required to reflect on the processes used and the artefacts that are produced. Schön describes how:

> In a good process of design, [the] conversation with the situation is reflective. In answer to the situation's back-talk, the designer reflects-in-action on the construction of a problem, the strategies of action, or the model of phenomena, which have been implicit in his moves. (79)

This "reflective designing," to use Schön's term, involves responding to problems that arise and using them to reframe the project and determine a way forward. It is this ability to work with problems in a reflective manner that defines a documentary designer.

18. The documentary designer understands that research is embedded in practice because they will often need to explore new ground.

A documentary designer is, to use Schön's argument, "a researcher in [a] practice context" (1983, 68). This concept means the documentary designer needs to be able to reflect on processes that occur as they happen, what Schön describes as "reflection-in-action." This helps the documentary designer to not be reliant on predetermined production approaches and concepts, instead the documentary designer is able to devise new ways of making and thinking as their practice unfolds. This is important for the documentary designer so they can work with the irregular specificities of interactive documentary design and production.

19. The documentary designer iteratively designs tools and production frameworks for these tools.

The tools that are used to make interactive documentaries create and require the formulation of what I refer to as "production frameworks" that work with the constraints of the tools used. Each tool is designed to function differently in regards to scripting, recording, editing, designing, and publishing documentaries. In the same way that it is important to understand the technical limits of different types of video cameras to meet the conceptual and technical requirements of a project, so too does the documentary designer need to remain open and flexible towards how digital tools are used in relation to previous documentary practices.

20. The documentary designer understands how to use sketches to iteratively explore possibilities, to probe and question options, and to make connections that define nuances for further refined development in order to determine how something might be achieved.

For the documentary designer a digital artefact produced as a sketch becomes a reference point for critique and provides ideas for further development. The documentary designer needs to engage with screen-based design, this includes the processes used in interaction design to create digital artefacts. Buxton (2007) argues that sketches are an expendable and agile form that can be used to test ideas and make discoveries within a design process.

21. The documentary designer uses prototypes, in real world environments, to determine whether something works and how it can be improved.

Prototyping provides a way to scope out an interactive work and test it with users, along with defining a project within set production constraints. As Dunbar states:

> Prototyping can be seen as a way in which designers and developers can collaboratively shape an interactive system in close contact with the digital materials, allowing an interaction design project to put an interactive system out into the world for people to experience. (2009, 126)

The prototype as an incomplete form of interactive media enables the practitioner to refine all aspects of an interactive documentary including interface design, user experience, documentary structure, narrative design, and how users will engage with the work, before committing to a final version.

A principle overarching all of these propositions for interactive documentary practice is dexterity. Dexterity is the ability to adjust to change in a responsive and fluid way. A documentary designer needs dexterity to be open and responsive toward embracing new technologies and ways of doing things to conduct documentary practice in a critical way. Future practice will require this dexterity.

Conclusion

In the transition to the new skills and knowledge required of the documentary designer there is the potential to utilise existing practice methodologies in documentary, including techniques such as storyboarding, camera tests, and pilot productions. However, the shift to design methodologies like sketching and prototyping digital artefacts, along with exploring works that are multilinear, involves an approach that is open towards exploring experimental options. In many cases outcomes are developed collaboratively through a design process involving clients, interaction designers, and users, and is dependent on the varying conditions of each project. This is a process that requires a combination of design and media practices to successfully produce content for publication online.

Documentary practitioners require a new set of skills and knowledge to work with interactive documentary online if they wish to practice within the dynamic and technology-driven domains of the Internet. This means that the documentary designer requires some understanding of user experience and interaction design as part of working with specialists such as interaction designers, web developers, and programmers.

By naming this documentary practice documentary design, I am recognising that documentary practice is in a continual state of redefinition in response to the development of new technologies. A documentary designer approaches the production of a documentary through a collaborative process of investigating suitable solutions relative to the particular requirements of each project. This shift in approach toward designing a documentary is important because the production of interactive digital media on the Internet involves more than just content creation. The transformation required to design for the lean-forward user in interactive documentary involves the documentary designer working as a co-creator, rather than the auteur common in traditional documentary production. The use of design thinking can inform the development of interactive documentary through the process of problem solving collaboratively with the audience. This collaborative approach allows the audience to be more directly involved in the process of creating a work.

Bibliography

Bas, Berke, and Florian Thalhofer. *Planet Galata: A Bridge in Istanbul*, 2010, Web.

Bordwell, David, and Kristin Thompson. *Film Art: An Introduction*. 9th ed. New York: McGraw-Hill, 2010.

Brachet, A., and A. Szalat. *Gaza Sderot*, 2008, Web.

Brooks, Kevin M. "Do Story Agents Use Rocking Chairs? The Theory and Implementation of One Model for Computational Narrative." *Proceedings of Multimedia '96*. Boston: ACM Press, 1996. 317–328.

Buchanan, Richard. "Wicked Problems in Design Thinking." *Design Issues* 8.2 (1992): 5–21.

Buxton, Bill. *Sketching User Experiences*. San Francisco: Morgan Kaufmann, 2007.

Crossover Labs. "Korsakow – Not the Linear-Causal Way of Thinking." *Crossover Labs*, January 1, 2015, Web.

Douglas, J. Yellowlees. *The End of Books or Books Without End?: Reading Interactive Narratives*. Ann Arbor: University of Michigan Press, 1999.

Dovey, Jon, and Mandy Rose. "We're Happy and We Know It: Documentary: Data: Montage." *Studies in Documentary Film* 6.2 (2012): 159–173.

Dressen, Arnaud, et al. *Klynt*. Computer Program. Paris, France: Honkytonk Films, 2012.

Dufresne, David, and Philippe Brault. *Prison Valley*. 2010, Web.

Dunbar, Michael. "Beyond Skin Deep: Exploring the Contribution of Communication Design Within Interaction Design Projects." RMIT University, M.Des. Thesis, 2009.
Gaudenzi, Sandra. *The Living Documentary: From Representing Reality to Co-creating Reality in Digital Interactive Documentary*. Goldsmiths, University of London, PhD Thesis, 2013.
Kimbell, Lucy. "Rethinking Design Thinking: Part 1." *Design and Culture* 3.3 (2011): 285–306.
Manovich, Lev. *The Language of New Media*. Cambridge, MA: MIT Press, 2001.
Manovich, Lev. "The Practice of Everyday (Media) Life." *Video Vortex Reader: Responses to Youtube*. Ed. Geert Lovink and Sabine Niederer. Amsterdam: XS4ALL, 2008. 33–44.
Merrin, William. "Studying Me-Dia: The Problem of Method in a Post-broadcast Age." *Media Studies 2.0*, 2010, Web.
Miles, Adrian. "Softvideography: Digital Video as Postliterate Practice." *Small Tech: The Culture of Digital Tools*. Ed. Byron Hawk, David M. Rieder and Ollie Oviedo. Minneapolis: University of Minnesota Press, 2008a. 10–21.
Miles, Adrian. "Programmatic Statements for a Facetted Videography." *Video Vortex Reader: Responses to Youtube*. Ed. Geert Lovink and Sabine Niederer. Amsterdam: XS4ALL, 2008b. 223–230.
Mozilla. *Popcorn Maker*. Computer Program. Mozilla, 2010.
Murray, Janet Horowitz. *Inventing the Medium: Principles of Interaction Design as a Cultural Practice*. Cambridge: MIT Press, 2012.
Nash, Kate. "Modes of Interactivity: Analysing a Webdoc." *Media, Culture and Society* 34.2 (2012): 195–210.
Nielsen, Jakob. "Writing Style for Print vs. Web." *Nielsen Norman Group*, 2008, Web.
Norman, Donald. *The Design of Everyday Things*. New York: Basic Book, 1998.
Norman, Donald. "Affordance, Conventions and Design (Part 2)." *Don Norman: Designing for People*, 1999, Web.
O'Flynn, Siobhan. "Documentary's Metamorphic Form: Webdoc, Interactive, Transmedia, Participatory and Beyond." *Studies in Documentary Film* 6.2 (2012): 141–157.
Plantinga, Carl R. *Rhetoric and Representation in Nonfiction Film*. Cambridge: Cambridge University Press, 1997.
Rowe, Peter. *Design Thinking*. Cambridge: MIT Press, 1998.
Ryan, Marie-Laure. "Beyond Myth and Metaphor: Narrative in Digital Media." *Poetics Today* 23.4 (2002): 581–609.
Ryan, Marie-Laure. *Narrative Across Media: The Languages of Storytelling*. Lincoln: University of Nebraska Press, 2004.
Schön, Donald. *The Reflective Practitioner*. London: Ashgate, 1983.

Soar, Matt. "Making (with) the Korsakow System: Database Documentaries as Articulation and Assemblage." *New Documentary Ecologies*. Ed. Kate Nash, Craig Hight and Catherine Summerhayes. Hampshire: Palgrave Macmillan, 2014. 154–173.

Soar, Matt, and Florian Thalhofer, "Release Notes." *Korsakow: The Next Level Story*, 2005, Web.

Thackara, John. *In the Bubble: Designing a Complex World*. Cambridge: MIT Press, 2005.

Thalhofer, Florian. *Korsakow*. Computer Program, 2000.

Ambient Media Making, Auto-Documentary, and Affect

Adrian Miles

Abstract This chapter describes a variety of emerging apps and platforms that constitute new forms of vernacular nonfiction. These apps and platforms create informal media trails as part of our mediated everyday. When considered as systems these apps provide a model for a yet to be realised mode of "auto-documentary" that aggregates events through what are described as automatic and ambient media machines.

Keywords Interactive documentary • Social media • Assemblage theory • Media materialism

Take One

This chapter is a consideration of interactive documentary from the point of view of affect. This is based on the use of Bergson's sensory motor schema that Deleuze undertakes in *Cinema One* (1986) to define the movement image. Within the movement image the affect image offers a model for interactivity, which I use as the basis from which to speculate

A. Miles (✉)
School of Media and Communication, RMIT University,
Melbourne, VIC, Australia

A. Miles (ed.), *Digital Media and Documentary*,
https://doi.org/10.1007/978-3-319-68643-1_5

about, and advocate for a form of interactive documentary that relies upon what I characterise as "affective interactivity."

Take Two

This is an essay that, in the spirit of digital intellectual maverick Ted Nelson, can be considered as an example of his portmanteau "thinkertoy." It has two halves, each of which may be incommensurable with the other. One half thinks about smart phones and their media apps as documentation practices. The other half thinks about affect as a desired function and purpose for these documentation practices in relation to nonfiction. The first half describes what we are currently doing, while the second speculates on what we could do. Both halves regard the things involved in smart phones, mobile media and documentation as constellations of machines. These machines, as Bryant defines them, "are composed of units or individual entities existing at a variety of different levels of scale, and that are themselves composed of other entities" where "entities dynamically operate on inputs producing outputs" (2014, 6). I take this description of machines as having affinities to the actor–network theory of Latour (2005), the assemblages described by Bennett (2010), and even Bogost's unit operations (2006). Machines, as systems assembled from parts that do things, is theoretically useful because when we meet a machine we tend to pay more attention to what it does, rather than what it means. Machine becomes then a useful conceit as it avoids letting the constellation of smart phones, mobile media, and documentation being only "a matter of language or some other form of cultural representation" (Barad, 81), for these machines are things that do. This is a chapter that begins to argue for future possibilities of these machines in the context of nonfiction as much as it is an accounting of current practices. To the extent that this chapter's two halves remain incommensurable their ill discipline is embraced as an unruly, scholarly, writing. It builds upon Dovey and Rose's valuable and intriguing observation that "[c]lassical documentary might be understood as a product of the 'age of steam' a form that evolved from the mechanical optical technologies of the nineteenth century" (160), accepting their implicit invitation to consider what a non-classical documentary in this internet age might be.

The Two Types of Media Machines

We are in the midst of networks of emerging mobile media practices that are creating informal, everyday, rich media forms of documentation. These mobile practices rely on apps that are, from the point of view of their developers, services, while for us as their end users these apps appear as relatively seamless *mediations* of our everyday activities—aspiring to provide what the corporate digital vernacular describes as a "friction free" experience. As services these apps and their attendant practices require the integration of the discrete parts that make up smart phones, Application Programming Interfaces (APIs), wireless telecommunications infrastructure, cables, electricity, the World Wide Web, Wi-Fi, code, and people, all relying on numerous technical standards and protocols. This integration makes it trivial for someone to now document, in situ, their world and to collate and curate this documentation into personal collections to be shared with audiences. These technologies, networks, and practices form what I think of as media machines. These machines currently work in two distinct ways.

The first, which we are probably most familiar with, mirror and augment existing media practices because they imitate legacy media. Examples of these apps and services include Instagram, Vine, Twitter, and Flickr. These media machines combine the smart phone as a recording device, with a dedicated app and a sophisticated service architecture that uses the Internet, World Wide Web, and APIs to facilitate what we now recognise as social media. These machines facilitate aggregation, curation, and real time sharing. These I describe as *documenting media machines* as they rely on a deliberate, intentional making—you choose to open Instagram, take a photograph, and share it. The second variety of media machine are not deliberate or intentional, and rely on the smart phone as an automatic sensor and aggregator. These media machines I describe as *ambient media machines* and examples include Moves, Momento, Reporter, and Saga.

Documenting Media Machines

The apps and services that perform as documenting media machines are most commonly used in informal, everyday media practices. This everyday quality has affinities with older traditions of personal documentation through informal media practices such as diary writing (van Dijck 2007). We photograph, note, and film the significant and banal as documented everyday acts of curiosity, ennui, joy, wonder, despair, boredom, and intrigue. As we record and share this media, finding our own valencies amongst it, we are also continuing technical media's mechanical and indifferent indexical recording of the world, for while we care, more or less, about what we film and photograph, our recording machine's care not a jot.

The media artefacts created using these apps document highlights and the mundane as they create an everyday media vernacular that is marked, absolutely, by our deliberate intent. I choose to write, photograph, video some *thing*, and to this extent these, and all similar services, have an affinity to previous media forms and practices where the artefacts created require deliberate actions to be realised—moral panics about their apparent triviality notwithstanding.

The phrase "documenting media machine" retains the sense of the indexical quality that technical media has as it mechanically and mathematically goes about recording things in the world. As Parikka argues, "it is the calculation- and number-logic-based ontology of technical (and especially computational) media through which cultural memory gets articulated" (2011, 57), and this, combined with our noticing, is what is realised here as an informal documenting. What becomes noticed, in each case, becomes a discrete media artefact, for example, a photograph on Instagram, and these noticed things in turn become events within these documenting media machines through likes, sharing, embedding, and other forms of endorsement. While these apps and services do document an individual's noticed world, their imperative is archival, rather than discursive, as they do not have the intentional articulating of an argument that documentary generally achieves through selection, reordering, and montage.

Documenting media machines then are a practice that lies between the deliberate and extroverted engagement that documentary offers with the world and the self-reflective and introspective self-noticing that underwrites diary traditions in writing and film. Documenting media machines rely on networked and computational protocols to allow our individual media artefacts that we have made to be interrogated, reused, embedded, and cited, where it is now technically simple to build services that through either human, or machine, curation incorporate these media artefacts from other sources as they are published. This type of re-integration of personal media making from one network to somewhere else is relied upon, for example, in the interactive documentary *18 Days in Egypt* (Mehta and Elayat 2011) where social media about the Egyptian Revolution is harvested for content. More recently, Gaudenzi's experimental *Digital Me* (2015), and Harris and Hochmuth's *Network Effect* (2015) also rely upon sourcing the media of others, from elsewhere, to algorithmically, aesthetically, and critically auto curate our artefactual media trails into fuzzy collections as generative new works.

Ambient Media Machines

A second type of media machine is an ambient media machine. Such machines are made up of media apps and services that create media artefacts that are no longer phenomenologically deliberate or intentional. As ambient media machines these apps and services are distinguished from the artefact-centred practices of documenting media machines such as Instagram and Vine by their symbiotic integration of the computational affordances of their host devices, the mobile web, and their always on status. These apps, for example, Memento, Moves, Reporter, Day One, and Saga, currently fall into two broad categories. One category are those ambient media machines that generate content and artefacts on their own, and the other are automatic aggregators of other documenting and ambient media machines. Each category of ambient media machine performs with the same technical indifference of prior technical media, yet unlike intentional media making they largely operate of their own accord, without needing a human to deliberately and intentionally select what, when, and where to record. (To this extent they are much closer to what we understand surveillance media to be.) As an example consider Moves. This is an iOS and Android app that, when activated, relies on local Wi-Fi, GPRS, and GPS to continuously track your mobile phone's movement. It provides a daily summary of this movement as an infographic, dividing movement into exercise-based activities, for example, walking, running, and cycling, and the more sedentary driving and public transport. Each day's movements are drawn using your mobile phone's default mapping application, and the types of movement and their associated locations can be user edited. Moves defines itself as an "Activity Diary," and as a self-described diary participates in the tradition of the diary as an observational, intimate, and personal form of documentation—today I walked so many steps and cycled this many kilometres to and from these locations.

The second category of ambient media machine, which shares some of the qualities of these automatic ambient machines, automatically collects media artefacts and data from other apps and services to collate them into messy collections. These aggregations of artefacts are commonly structured through the use of a simple timeline to orientate us to its cluttered parts.

Many of these ambient aggregators are part of the "quantified self" movement, a digital lifestyle culture that enjoys recording personal data to then apply a variety of metrics for the "sculpting" of self-defined lifestyle choices. For example, the web-based service Exist allows you to "track everything in one place, understand your life" as it aggregates data from a wide range of other services to then algorithmically identify significant patterns to, in the language of personal productivity, "enhance" your habits.

Apps such as Moves, while signalling the rise of personal ambient media, are, like the earlier intentional media-making apps Instagram and Vine, orientated to one key function. However, the Software Development Kit (SDK) of mobile phones include APIs that allow apps like Moves to share the data it collects with other apps. This allows for the aggregation of data from different ambient media machines to build a different type of media machine. An example of an app that undertakes this type of automatic aggregation is Momento. Within Momento you can configure a number of "feeds" from other intentional media machines including Flickr, Instagram, blogs, as well as ambient media machines such as Moves. Momento *automatically* collects data and artefacts from these services and curates them into a date-arranged collection. To supplement this harvesting Momento also invites you to define prompts that encourage self-reporting throughout the day.

Momento is an example of what are commonly known as life journaling apps. Momento auto-aggregates the pieces of media from other intentional and ambient apps that are documenting the everyday and automatically combines my photographs, blog posts, and Facebook status updates with location and movement history from Moves. Momento becomes a machine that entangles media loosely around my self and this automatic loose entangling inaugurates what I am tentatively naming auto-documentary. ("Auto" here serves a useful double duty, indicating the "automatic" of the rule-governed machine and the Greek "autos" of the self.)

Such auto-documentaries collect the chatter from ambient media machines to create thick media palimpsests. These palimpsests are braided from what would otherwise be the discrete and separate media trails created through the mix of deliberate media making and the indifferent recording of activities by my smart phone as an ambient sensor. This automatic recording of worldly movements, at first glance, seems to erase any possibility for considered judgement or reflection as it dissolves decision making into the machine's automaticity, begging the question of their value and relevance to documentary. However, if we consider their combining of intended media documentation and ambient media trails using

Deleuze's concept of the affect image a material account of what these documenting machines do becomes available. From the point of view of these machines *our* use of them sees us as operating as a Deleuzean affective interval, a living centre, around which these machines fold. Using this Deleuzean concept of the affective interval these machines can then be understood to introduce a pause and interval into the everyday. This pause, as an interruption or hesitation, always has the possibility of enlarging itself, in time, around me as its indeterminate, living centre. As Deleuze argues:

> For Bergson, the gap, the interval, will be sufficient to define one type of image among others, but a very special type—living images or matters [matières]. Whereas the other images act and react on all their facets and in all their parts, here we have images which only receive actions on one facet or in certain parts and only execute reactions by and in other parts. (1986, 61)

In the case of ambient media machines this centre has the possibility to no longer be an ego grounded in a deliberate making but is the consequence and effect of the aggregation of diverse media artefacts generated as my trail. To the extent that this trail and an auto-documentary machine are produced I am the relational effect or consequence of these medias, not the other way round—they, relationally, construct me as the result of their epicycles. The implications of these braided media assemblages for interactive documentary is in the automaticity of affect that they might engender, document, or enable. In what, to use Deleuze's cinema philosophy, have the potential to become interactive affect images precisely by virtue of their indifferent technical documenting of moments that can come to matter, and in this mattering provide moments of hesitation and therefore consideration.

Reprise (and Pivot)

In my pocket I have a phone. In my phone there is a video camera, GPS, and microcomputer. We have witnessed and are experiencing a revolution in media making with the rise of mobile media platforms and services. These apps and services, such as Instagram and Vimeo, rely on an intentional or deliberate making of individual media artefacts by individuals that then find themselves serialised or aggregated into collections. However, we are also now seeing the development of new applications and services that reconceptualise the smart phone as an automatic, non-intentional media *instrument*. This instrument is always on, producing an everyday, indifferent, and indirect media recording. An ambient media making. This shift in the use of mobile phones from a ready-to-hand networked media tool to an automatic and indifferent media machine has implications for how we might understand and develop interactive documentary.

Smart phones as ambient media machines herald the emergence of nonfiction forms that automatically interweave media trails and the everyday. This is achieved through the use of apps that take advantage of their network awareness, combined with an algorithmic automaticity, that is a movement away from the screen as the privileged site of media making toward what I characterise as an "ambient auto-documentary." These ambient apps, for example, Reporter, Saga, and Momento, aggregate and curate the real-time media trails that form through our mobile devices. This automatic aggregating and curating shifts the role of technical media away from a deliberate documentation—I photograph, write, and film—toward one that facilitates the production of machine networks that are created in the wake of our lived, post digital, experiences. Ambient auto-documentary is distributed amongst the services, servers, apps, mobile handsets, protocols, and people that it emerges from, where an intentional media practice is secondary to this automatic and algorithmic curation of our media trails.

These apps and services grant an agency to the computer as a procedural machine, and in their use people become Latourian mediaries amongst these networks and flows of images, GPS coordinates, data, 3G, 4G, and Wi-Fi signals, text, video, platforms, and services. As nonfiction, ambient media machines seem to address the self *and* their technosocial assemblages where the self is now an interval between these machine's noticing and our own understanding. That is, a moment of affective indetermination.

Affect One: Affective Intervals

In *Cinema One* Gilles Deleuze outlines his concept of the movement image, which he derives from Bergson's sensory motor schema. In the movement image Deleuze offers a materialist account of perception where the world is made of up "images [that] act and react as a function of each other, on all their facets and all their parts" (1986, 62). Living things introduce a particular type of gap or interval amongst these acting and reacting facets that allows for movement images to have three major forms, the perception, action, and affect images. In film perception images arise when some things, rather than others, are noticed, that is they are subtracted from amongst everything else that could be noticed. What comes to be noticed in this way is a consequence of the 'interest' of the living centre—we notice what *might* matter to us—and for Deleuze this is realised cinematically as those shots, and even films, that emphasise noticing, where someone or something is watching and seeing. The action image becomes those shots and sequences in a film that are a response to what has been perceived or noticed. It is realised literally as an action to what has been perceived and is more broadly "our possible action on things" (Deleuze 1986, 65). The affect image falls between the automaticity of perception and action, between noticing and doing. It is characterised by Deleuze as a gap or interval between perception and action because the affect image interrupts the perceptual relay between perception and action, and is "a perception which is troubling … and a hesitant action" (1986, 65). Affect then requires a decision about the possible actions that could be undertaken in response to what has been noticed. However, importantly for Deleuze, affect is also that which remains in the body, unexpended, after such action. As Deleuze states, affection "is what occupies the interval … without filling it in or filling it up" (1986, 65) Affect is then that part of the sensory motor schema that remains after a decision has been enacted, and so has the opportunity to materially join thinking, consideration, action, and reflection. More simply, unlike the striving of perception and action; "more," "faster," "look," the affect image haunts; "why?", "how come?"

This tripartite schema of perception, action, and affect describes a material economy of action and reaction where consciousness is measured as the extent of the interval between perception and action. In such a sensory motor schema action arises as a consequence of perception, and strives to be an adequate answer or response to it. Affect, and the affect image, falls to one side of this economy of adequate noticing and doing because affect introduces uncertainty, indecision, and indeterminancy between the often automatic relays of perception and action.

This sensory motor schema provides an elegant heuristic by which to understand interactivity within interactive documentary. Just as the movement image in general is made up of perception, affect, and action we can understand interactivity as being made up of noticing, deciding, and doing. In this schema noticing is ceded to the interface as the site of display, while doing is realised as literal physical actions through swipes, taps, touches, and clicks. Decision, however, falls, in varying ways, between the computational and the user as a shared centre of indetermination.

When interactivity is considered using this Deleuzean typology affect can be understood as the privileged mode of interaction for interactive documentary because the interval associated with the affect image becomes the user's indecision as they are invited by a work to decide upon an action. By introducing a deliberate pause in the flow of media, a flow that can be re-enabled by a decision realised as an action by the user in the interface, this pause and its subsequent decision-as-action can have consequence in the work and therefore for the user. This consequence, I hope, is where the importance of affect for interactivity and auto-documentary lies for if the decisions based on my perceiving and acting alters the form or shape of the work then my relation to a work is now situated and constituted as this relational, affective, interval.

Affect Two: Affective Interactivity

Bergson's sensory motor schema and Deleuze's cinematic movement image therefore offers an elegant account of interactivity for interactive documentary. What comes to be noticed in a work, when and how, is facilitated by an interface that lets users make decisions. These decisions are literally realised as motor actions. These actions, in turn, effect a change in the work that becomes visible through the interface and these changes are in turn noticed, inviting something new to be decided, and then acted upon. This iterative schema is one of noticing, deciding, and doing.

Using this schema we can understand that interactive documentaries that are encyclopaedic or archival tend to emphasise content and navigation and so become particularly concerned with usability. Such interactive documentaries are aligned to the perception image. Interactive documentaries that require manual dexterity, puzzle solving, "levelling up," and badges are aligned to the action image. These works emphasise and reward the rapidity of decision making and action. Works that are less interested in the encyclopaedic, or in quick decision making, move toward the affect image. Such affective interactive documentaries allow for a deliberate and considered noticing that offers the time to *wonder* about what to do. Such an affective interactivity lends itself to themes, content, structures, and material that is associative and poetic. Affective interactivity then offers an emotional and epistemological economy for interactive documentary that has affinities with the essay, for affect in these contexts allows what are otherwise automatic and unnoticed moments to become interrupted and slowed for consideration. It is in this interruption and noticing that affective interactivity affords the opportunity for an expanded consideration of the world in interactive documentary. The user's role and agency in relation to a work becomes a material part of a discursive, documenting, perceptual, machine. As a user in an affective interactive work we are neither centre nor margin but a relational actor required to notice, consider, and act where what we can decide to do has import for the work ontologically, returning us to new situations of question and concern.

A Poetics of Affective Interactivity

The affect image as a slow interval, an indeterminancy that falls between noticing and doing, therefore offers a novel way to conceive of an interactive documentary poetics. It suggests that interactive documentary, while certainly offering sociocultural critique, social engagement, or novel technocultural forms, can also interrupt, suspend, and slow the ideas, events, and problems that any interactive documentary addresses and responds to. This slowed interval is, partly, what the quantified self movement is undertaking—though they don't use these terms—as it seeks a qualitative understanding of the quantitative moments collected in its data. In the context of the documentary media machines discussed in this chapter my question is simple, even naive, and asks what might happen if we made documentary media machines from the point of view of an affective interactivity?, if indecision and indeterminancy were to became privileged terms in making and understanding? (The affect image as a slow interval also has the benefit of letting us be cautious about the excitement generated by the first wave of interactive documentary where the ability to combine, link, and present media in multilinear ways risks becoming only a celebration of technical spectacle.)

A poetics of affective interactivity lets us recognise that affect offers a non-didactic, materialist, and qualitative engagement with the world for interactive documentary. Affect offers opportunities to enlarge, slow down, and otherwise *interrupt* and make noticeable the everyday. Such noticing, through affective interactivity, is a preliminary step toward media machines that help us recognise the intensive in the everyday. This concept of affective interactivity is a productive heuristic when applied to the emerging app systems and networks happening around us. These systems and networks are complicated socio–technical networks which can be reconceived as affective machines for the creation of intervals of considered noticing within the everyday. This is, speculatively, their import for documentary. That is, interactivity in interactive documentary, ambient media machines, and auto-documentaries are affective rather than representational systems. They do, rather than narrate or explain, with a trail of meaning arising later in their wake.

For a Cyborg Documentary

These are speculative ideas to think about the intersection of gadgetry, networks, and audiovisual nonfiction that is happening around us. I want to imagine a future documentary platform that curates my intentional documenting on Instagram, Flickr, Twitter, and Facebook and braids this with material from my automatic ambient media machines. What sort of personal documentation or documentary is this? What authorial actions or interventions, and when, are necessary for such machines to become affective auto-documentary machines and not just aggregators? Is this what documentary and big data would look like?

As these new media tools, apps, and services become increasingly porous to each other through the standardisation of protocols the media artefacts we produce become, in turn, more pliable, their edges softening and blurring, as once discrete instances—this photo from that time—become mediaries within ever shifting patterns of relation. This possible mixing of an automatic ambient media making with intentional technical media offers methods for possible future interactive documentary practices and systems.

Rather than thinking about what sorts of assemblages or networks are formed by these practices, equipment, technologies, and protocols, and how these might enhance ethnographic, observational, essayist, or direct cinema practices, it is the implications of these assemblages for future forms of documentary that interests me.

I can imagine a documentary machine network that auto-curates individual media artefacts into categories, allowing multiple ways for these artefacts and categories to be searched, presented, navigated, and interpreted. Geodata could be used to map this media, and algorithms would identify patterns that emerge autopoietically amongst this flow, creating interactive documentary works that, as Gaudenzi suggests, are "open systems (systems that can change themselves, and to a certain degree, can create themselves)" (2013, 26). A platform operating in this way would be an ongoing, quintessentially unfinished autopoietic documentary open to indeterminate and indefinite futures. Such a platform would be granular and porous, where even after curation of its individual parts, its videos, photographs, paragraphs, and sounds could be reused to make other patterns and relations, embedded elsewhere, woven into other projects, sites, and places. Such an open, evolving, and porous structure refashions and muddies the edges and definitions of documentary, and invites a mode of working that is aggregative, generative, procedural, and open, a model that allows for the crafting of patterned, emergent complexity.

This would be an interactive audiovisual nonfiction practice that allows affect within documentary through the creation of indeterminate intervals. As ambient and auto-documentary aggregates the records of the banal, novel, and important, affective interactivity will occur when our platforms and systems facilitate and invite the discovery of relations that matter amongst this material rather than the current interest in the documentation and presentation of extant knowledge. This allows for an affective and automatic interactive documentary machine that sees and participates in the world as an indeterminate and speculative site of investigation and knowing. A technosocial knowledge making and performing that might let us address the messy complexity of what is, rather than corralling it into the shapes demanded of our stories and tools. This would, I hope, be the point of and for any poetics of affective interactivity, and is what computational nonfiction media machines could do.

Bibliography

Bennett, Jane. *Vibrant Matter: A Political Ecology of Things*. Durham: Duke University Press, 2010.

Bogost, Ian. *Unit Operations: An Approach to Videogame Criticism*. Cambridge: The MIT Press, 2006.

Bryant, Levi R. *Onto-Cartography: An Ontology of Machines and Media*. Edinburgh: Edinburgh University Press, 2014.

Deleuze, Gilles. *Cinema One: The Movement–Image*. Trans. Hugh Tomlinson and Barbara Habberjam. Minneapolis: University of Minnesota Press, 1986.

Dovey, Jon, and Mandy Rose. "We're Happy and We Know It: Documentary, Data, Montage." *Studies in Documentary Film* 6.2 (2012): 159–173.

Exist - Understand Your Behaviour, 2017, Web.
Gaudenzi, Sandra. "The Interactive Documentary as a Living Documentary." *Doc On-Line: Digital Magazine on Documentary Cinema* 14 (2013): 9–31.
Gaudenzi, Sandra. "Digital Me." *Digital Me*, 2015, Web.
Harris, Jonathan, and Greg Hochmuth. *Network Effect*, 2015, Web.
Latour, Bruno. *Reassembling the Social: An Introduction to Actor-Network-Theory*. Oxford: Oxford University Press, 2005.
Mehta, Jigar, and Yasmin Elayat. *18 Days in Egypt*, 2011, Web.
Parikka, Jussi. "Operative Media Archaeology: Wolfgang Ernst's Materialist Media Diagrammatics." *Theory, Culture & Society* 28.5 (2011): 52–74.
Van Dijck, Jose. *Mediated Memories in the Digital Age*. Stanford: Stanford University Press, 2007.

Miniature and Series: The Re-invention of the Epistolary Form in the Work of Alexander Hahn

Cathie Payne

Abstract This chapter uses a case study to examine the video "miniature" as a documentary method to capture transient and ephemeral interactions as a particular conceptual and aesthetic strategy. It analyses the video vignettes of Alexander Hahn's *Bharat|India* blog (2012–2013) and *Indian Records (2013)*, seeing the vignettes as miniatures that re-invent the epistolary form more commonly seen in the scientific field diary, sketchbook, journal and travelogue. The video miniatures in the case study allow for an intimate, personal and reflexive practice and offers a way to reflect on the incongruities, strangeness, vastness and beauty of the world, within the context of accelerated urban density and a changing anthropogenic worldview.

Keywords Digital documentary • Digital media • Video art • Media arts • Social media • Alexander Hahn

For John Conomos and Helene de Burgh-Woodman.

C. Payne (✉)
School of Creative Industries, Faculty of Education and Arts, The University of Newcastle, Callaghan, NSW, Australia

A. Miles (ed.), *Digital Media and Documentary*,
https://doi.org/10.1007/978-3-319-68643-1_6

Finding how to discuss emergent ways of thinking and seeing the world in contemporary documentary and media art raises the question of the efficacy of particular analytical and critical systems to engage with innovative works, as well as the types of works these systems privilege. This is particularly relevant in the study of work by filmmakers and artists who experiment and transform documentary materials, genres, media, and modes. Philosopher Michel Serres has, for instance, cautioned against the use of a "single passkey" and the "readymade solutions proffered by a particular method" whether psychoanalytical, phenomenological, epistemological, Marxist or semiotic, and advocates the necessity to "leap aside," so as not to preclude "local detail": invention and singularities that may unearth new ways of seeing (Serres 1995, 89–91). His advice offers a way to feel in the dark, to draw connections across disciplines that are increasingly problematised by the profound shift in ecological, geological and biological worldviews, and its consequences. In this chapter I use a method of detailed description to map the new phenomena of what I call the "media art trail." Such a media art trail is evident in a long-form video work called *Indian Records* (2013) by Swiss–German, New York-based media artist Alexander Hahn, and its related video blog site, *Bharat|India* (2012–2013). This long-form video and blog are composed of a series of very short videos that capture the minutiae of everyday life in India and are *perceptual acts* that offer a new method of encounter between the documentary media maker and the world. I propose that Hahn's method of engaging with the very small, the fleeting, and the momentary, is part of an intimate, deeply personal and reflexive practice that offers a way to reapproach the world through this change of scale—a world in miniature—and to reflect on this strangeness, vastness and beauty of what is found within the context of a changing anthropogenic worldview.

Alexander Hahn has worked at the forefront of the electronic and digital media arts in Europe and America for more than thirty years. A master's graduate of Zurich University, Hahn's twenty single-channel video works, and thirty-four multi-channel installations since 1977 have been exhibited in more than nineteen solo exhibitions and thirty group exhibitions and film festivals from New York to Locarno, Sydney to Berlin. His work draws from history, art, architecture, science and the labyrinths of western knowledge—its machines of sight and thought—and shuttles uneasily between a past and a future time. In his works the contemporary world—mental, physical, psychic, social, and geographical—appears to exist eerily between archaeology and mind map, a world describing a state of terminal decay and future possibility. Hahn's video and installation work is also characterised by a persistent engagement and experimentation with emergent image and sound-processing software and technologies, particularly in the use of electronic and digital imaging and sound techniques since the 1980s. His eclectic, multidisciplinary approach draws on experimental film, video, electro-acoustic, and 3D media art techniques, which he adapts for use in his videos and installations. In an earlier video work, *Dirt Site* (1990) surreal "landscapes" that are both interior and exterior transport the viewer between a poetic and metaphysical reality. The world in *Dirt Site* appears to be in various states of decay and efflorescence with mind and world in a complex intermix. The film is painstakingly constructed using image processing software to foreshadow a post-apocalyptic future, revealing a complex reflexive consciousness, and lay the foundation for Hahn's concerns in *Indian Records (2013).*

Hahn's *Bharat|India* blog and *Indian Records* are comprised of a series of very short videos that he labels "video vignettes." When these vignettes are collected they become an example of the contemporary reprisal of epistolary forms such as the scientific field diary, sketchbook, journal and travelogue, yet reinvented as an atomised and miniature form. The works link and connect media art and documentary practices to a larger history of documentation methods that underpins the hard and soft sciences, and are part of a new wave of media art that uses social media sites to collect and aggregate content (photo media, video and sounds) based on the artist or video maker's personal journey. Key works that use this modality include *maZine* (2009–2012) by Norwegian-based British artist Jeremy Welsh, *The Golden Tide* (2012–2013) by London-based artist Gayle Chong Kwan and *augment_me* (2009) by Australian media artist Brad Miller. Each of these works are examples of the relatively recent phenomenon that I have called the media art trail—a peripatetic and aleatory art form that reprises a range of short form video art, photomedia, documentary, literary, musical, and media art practices.

Social media sites such as Path, Vimeo, YouTube, WordPress, and Blogger, that have emerged since the mid-2000s, provide gateways and hubs for experimental media arts as they allow for the posting of short-form videos and series. In the hands of media artists such as Hahn these atomised and episodic cinematic pieces have reflexive, poetic, participatory, and revelatory potentials for mapping shifting perceptions of our relation to nature and the natural. In turn these social media sites have seeded the re-emergence and re-invention of short-form video and photography, not only as a "new cinema of attractions" (Rizzo 2008), but in the intimacy and reflexivity of micronarrative and their miniature forms. They provide avenues for experimental media art and new documentary forms that are poetic and short, in lieu of long form or "grand narratives" (Lyotard 1984, 15). These sites, as we shall see, give rise to new forms, perceptions and affects through such things as digital travelogues, diaries series, and trails that make sense of the things that "move us" (Ivakhiv 2013, 5).

The occurrence of media art trails has increased with the convergence of mobile smartphone technology and integrated high-speed mobile broadband since 2012. Hahn's recent works on India reflect not only the ubiquity of small digital video camera technology in everyday life but also the transformation of perceptions of nature in urban and the developing worlds. Hahn's work demonstrates that a social media art trail offers new possibilities for documenting journeys across the earth, and for bringing to consciousness some of the anthropogenic impacts that are part of contemporary accelerated urbanisation. Such work confronts us with questions about our relationships to the earth in the Anthropocene.

India Travelogue

During a three-month artist's residency in India, Hahn published his series of video vignettes on a video blog called *Bharat|India Travelogue|Video Vignettes* (2012–2013). This blog provides a record of Hahn's travels across the densely populated Indo–Gangetic plain that stretches from India's north-east to its north-west. This vast alluvial plain is bound by the Himalayas, fed by numerous rivers, and was successively home to the Bronze Age Indus Valley Civilisation, the ancient empire of the Gupta (320–550 CE), the Delhi Sultanate (1210–1526), the Mughal (1526–1857), and more recently British colonial rule and Independent India. The Indo–Gangetic plain is now threatened by controversial irrigation systems, silting rivers, overpopulation, sinking water tables, and water shortages (Acciavati 2015). Hahn's work logs fleeting video impressions of the "ordinary and nondescript" (Hahn 2013a) noticing human impact at very small scales as he travels through the urban spaces of New Delhi, the villages of McLeod Ganj and Sidhpur (the refuge place of the Dalai Lama and Tibetan diaspora), Dharamsala in the foothills of the Himalayas, and to the ancient backstreets and ghats (river steps) of Varanasi, returning by journey's end to New Delhi.

Hahn's vignettes were filmed between 29 September 2012 and 31 December 2012 and posted to the *Bharat|India* blog (2013a) at regular intervals. The result is an online travel diary of twenty-seven vignettes, each from thirty seconds to two-and-a-half minutes long. Each vignette reveals fleeting instants of everyday life captured on a portable camera from a bike, car, or while walking, as well as glimpses from, or into, apartments, domestic spaces, rooms, and public places. Hahn captures collisions between old and new worlds, cycles of urban and ecological renewal, breakdown and decay, and the co-existence of ancient practices with Western material culture such as urban toilets, plumbing systems, polluted roads, and street paths in ancient cities. Yet what also emerges in his video blog is a poetic and reflexive consciousness that reflects on "a society obsessed with recording and archiving everything" (Hahn 2013a).

Hahn subsequently compiled twenty-two videos of these vignettes into the long-form video work, *Indian Records* (2013b) posting it to Vimeo. Hahn describes *Indian Records* as, "[a] compilation of video vignettes, singular acts amidst the ordinary and the nondescript, caught by happenstance" (2013b).

For *Indian Records* Hahn separated each vignette by an intertitle and a piece of black leader. *Indian Records* provides fleeting episodic moments and insight into the experience of the senses when confronted with the immensity of urban density in northern India. As such, Hahn's work is a model that converges experimental documentary and media art modes and techniques with the serial capacities of online media to create a type of affective or perceptual breadcrumb that captures his encounters in India. His work is marked by a traveller's sense of perception as it oscillates between the very large—India—and the very small—moments in time. And, like the figure of Hermes who creates "*rapprochements*", connections between spaces and worlds, the works form a "flight pattern" through the multiple stratigraphies of space and time (Serres and Latour, 63–64).

Hahn describes an epiphany he experienced on his journey through India from which his initial concept for *Indian Records* sprang:

> A pivotal moment in my stay occurred on the day I was traveling by car from Delhi to Agra. The road appeared to me like a carpet that unrolled in a constant process of amazing genesis. Dust, gunk and colours emerged from the fallow light and momentarily congealed as people, fauna, flora and

> commodities—instants of evanescent life, each beautiful and unique, all too quickly fading in the rear view mirror. (2013b)

This rich, detailed, and intricate description through a car windshield is akin to Virilio's "dromoscopy" (2008). Dromoscopy describes the altered perception experienced while driving, the hallucinatory cinematic perception of life that results from the disintegration of matter, space, and time through speed (Virilio 2008, 101–116). Hahn's epiphany articulates a type of acceleration of human sensory perception where the cinematic and cinematographic converge in the drive between Delhi to Agra, and his description captures a sense of the fusion and entanglement of the senses that results from the experience of speed and travel. Yet Hahn also articulates a sense of the momentary and its inter-relationship with the vastness of space and time, organic and inorganic matter, and processes of transformation and renewal. In this "pivotal moment" *matter* and *energy* are intuited in a state of fusion—dust, people, plants, commodities congeal yet also appear interchangeable, *part of an unfolding procession*. This description verges on the dreamlike as Hahn describes this fusion as "instants of evanescent life." Physical, temporal and energetic entities appear to emerge distinctly for an instant, to then decay and fall back into the whole from which they came. As Virilio says "we live less in our own habitat (its field having practically disappeared) than in the habit of velocity" (2008, 116). It is this shift in perception between self and world, through transport, travel and encounter, as well as a reflexive observation of the connection and disconnection between people and their impact on the world, that Hahn maps in *Indian Records*. To look closely at this phenomenon, we will now turn to a detailed description, discussion, and analysis of Hahn's video vignettes.

Arrival in a New World

New Delhi, 29 September–23 October 2012

The opening series of video vignettes posted to the *Bharat|India* blog, and compiled in *Indian Records*, are recorded in the streets of New Delhi in northern India. These are a mix of video and sound art and experimental documentary. Each vignette has an enigmatic title that provides a reflexive clue, ironic reference, double entendre or pun as Hahn captures nondescript moments, places, and things. The titles—"Spectral Figures," "The

Beauty of Traffic Jams," "Fake Rain," and "Tectonic Shifts"—serve as their own perceptual trail and are entry points into the micro-worlds glimpsed in New Delhi by the curious traveller and his independent camera-eye.

The first vignette, "Spectral Figures," introduces the viewer to a poetics of arrival, banality and estrangement reminiscent of a traveller's encounter with a new city at night. An ancient electric light strobes and flickers outside a fairground, accompanied by an eerie, reverberating soundtrack. In a single take the camera pans across a cracked and peeling wall, with a man holding a plastic bottle near a sign that says "Toilet" and "Drinking Water," to reveal a sleeping dog prostrate on the warm stone tiles bathed in an eerie cadmium yellow light. Each of the elements of the vignette contributes to a sense of alienation—a glimpse of a city in decay. In "Butterfly Effect" (on the *Bharat|India* blog only) Hahn captures a moment from a sightseeing trip to the Mughal Emperor Humayun's tomb, captured in daylight through the viewfinder of a digital camera. Here Hahn creates a *rapprochement* between past and present. The ancient tomb coexists for a fraction of a second with the glint of light on a plastic butterfly clip in a young girl's hair. In "Night Cycle" the camera person's invisible presence lingers in a night garden, offering a strange respite amongst the sounds of beeps, honks, horns and the murmur of city traffic in the distance. In "Brass Advisory" the warped reflections of the camera person/traveller are captured momentarily in the brass plate on the wall of the International Association of Sound and Audio-Visual Archives. These various small acts of reflexivity by the artist recur throughout the work.

Each vignette reflects the author's humour in the miasma and hyper-vigilance of the senses while travelling as well as its banality, amidst the labyrinths and alienating backstreets of the city. There are disorientating moments, such as in "Juice Stand" where soapsuds drip down from the blue canvas of a juice stand in New Delhi; the patter of water on a neighbour's awning in "Fake Rain"; the ripple of a rickshaw driver's shirt bathed in orange light in "Tectonic Shifts" a futuristic metro station bathed in dust and smog in "Beauty of Traffic Jams"; and the disorientating view of a transaction at an ATM from the bottom of a well of water accompanied by the gurgling and shunting of an ancient plumbing system in "Aqueous Transfer Machine."

Each vignette is realised as a miniature long take, capturing a continuous scene, separated by lengths of black leader that fade in and out like the opening and closing of a curtain or a theatre's lights. Through this attention to otherwise prosaic moments and things the creation of micro-worlds is achieved by enlarging these moments and things. For instance, in a sequence from *Indian Records* that comprises "Fake Rain 1," "Fake Rain 2," and "Juice Stand," Hahn places the camera in a gutter, on a window ledge and on a juice stand, respectively. He records the drips and splats of water falling on the camera from the leaky air-conditioning unit in a New Delhi backstreet and the trajectory of liquid from a juice stand in the central market. The non-human and machine perspectives captured in these three vignettes contribute to a sense of disorientation as the viewer struggles to situate themselves and the images in space and time. The viewer is also pressed to consider the micro-impacts of human occupation through this concentration on the materiality of such everyday things as unmaintained cooling systems as Hahn shares his struggle to make sense of the urban sounds in his new surroundings. For example, in "Fake Rain 1" a poetic opening text tells us:

> Around 5h30 am, I sometimes wake up to the sound of rain. *Fooled again*, I'm thinking to myself as I listen to the patter of water on the nextdoor neighbor's awning. A few flights up, the spin cycle of a washing machine sets in. The servants have started their day. (Hahn, "Fake Rain 1", 2013b)

Here Hahn captures through images, sound, and text the concentration and awareness of detail of the observant, watchful traveller, noticing and filtering the dense proximity of people in urban spaces. In "Fake Rain 2," as the camera captures a drop of water falling from an awning, we can hear the splat of a single drop—it becomes a monumental event—as we wait to hear the next. Hahn transforms the everyday into the sublime through slow motion and colour as the single droplet glides over the surface of the lens, and with rising anticipation, we await the next. We see the droplet slowed down in time, a complete world in itself. Prosaic images are now transformed into micro–aesthetic moments, just as the aerial and corner of a rooftop become blurred and strange, lines etched into an aqua sky.

This micro–aesthetic sensibility is continued in the "Beauty of Traffic Jams" as Hahn uses a long take to capture the unearthly world of a city underpass near a metro station during peak hour. The metro, part of the beating heart of New Delhi's massive transport system, is a world of urban materials: metal, chrome, cement, tar, and incandescent and halogen headlights. The threshold which Hahn invites the viewer to enter is via a hand held camera from a car window caught in a traffic jam. In this world of superhighways and overpasses the geometries of concrete, dust, and light mix. There are glimpses of passing cars as they flicker and slide into the night. A dream of life unfolds in the shot: the drift of passers-by, the shadow play of silhouettes of plants like a memory of the future, with the hulls and husks of cars moving across the metallic bridge, curving like a crest of a wave. This is a landscape of indecipherability, somewhere between dream, science fiction and a future present. Hahn's metro station reveals a barely, yet all too recognisable, urban nature.

In vignettes such as "Tectonic Shifts," "Shadow in Motion Sketch 1" and "Shadow in Motion Sketch 2," the long take is a handheld shot from the back of a motorbike, briefly capturing the world as it passes by. Each of these vignettes is a single take of between thirty seconds and two minutes, and they form part of the aesthetic structure and larger journey cycles used in both *Indian Records* and the *Bharat|India* blog. The shots are augmented by the video maker/camera person/traveller, as he swings, moves, and zooms with the handheld camera. The camera records continuously, part of the moment of performance in these "singular acts" (2013b). Here Hahn mercilessly captures the relationships between the human, the urban and the world: an intermix of earth and species, car exhaust and rubber tyres, yesterday's garbage strewn by chickens and dogs, and the crushed matter from the wheels of motorbikes that integrates into the streets of the city.

Through the use of the miniature long take Hahn remediates the aleatory and peripatetic wanderings of Baudelaire's *flaneur* (1863) or the drift and encounter characterised by French theorist and Situationist Guy Debord. It is a way of documenting the minutiae of everyday shifts and changes in the city as it converges with global capitalism. Hahn uses the digital camera as a robotic object to interact, record and reflexively engage with the world. It becomes an augmented, alien camera-eye that sees things in space and time from all angles and directions. A roving camera-eye that can be left or placed anywhere—from the ground or suspended from great heights, set in motion while commuting on buses, trains, cars and bikes—and enables a topological vision, made possible through an active optic; the sight machines of cinema, video and computer graphics (Virilio 1989). In this way, moments from everyday life in *Indian Records* become the object of an alien and digital vision as Hahn selects insect and bird like perspectives, as if non-human eyes were gazing out at the early twenty-first century back lots of New Delhi and Varanasi, portending an automated, intelligent robotic future.

Varanasi, City of light

1–27 November 2012

Hahn's next sequence of vignettes are filmed in Varanasi. Varanasi is a sacred and luminous city that is "older than history" (Twain 1897, 480), and one of the oldest living cities in the world (Singh 2011, 205–206). Its architecture, an outcome of the continuous cultural and religious traditions of Hinduism, Buddhism, Islam, Sikhism, Jainism, and pilgrimage (Singh, 217), lies at the confluence of the Varuna and the Assi rivers. The Assi, today, is reduced to a "drain, full of sludge, plastic and litter" (Dhillon 2014) among the suburbs, tourist apartments, and student houses, but Assi Ghat, the place where the Assi meets the great Ganges River, remains a sacred place. Students and tourists now occupy the steps that descend into the river, where, as Dhillon notes, "to bathe in the Ganges is to wash away your sins," yet now the river mirrors the polluted conditions of the city itself, as raw sewage, chemicals, human remains, and waste are dumped into its waters (Dhillon 2014). Up-river, a multitude of shrines and temples stretch tier after tier along the water's edge. The city itself echoes the labyrinthine shape of the river and appears to have emerged over millennia, from the alluvial soil it was built on, to be part of the bones of the earth itself. Sediment now chokes the river. Numerous dams, combined with the illegal drawing of water, pollution, and refuse have reduced its flow, creating sandbars like varicose veins wearing down the river with little promise of renewal.

Hahn's vignettes of Varanasi take us into the backstreets to find the sacred in the small things that are part of the everyday. In "Trophic Levels in the Food Chain" a man sits cross-legged on the pavement as a bird flies against a blue sky amidst the cacophony of crowds, people and birdcalls. Hahn's images here are a composite of earth and sky as an image of constancy amongst relentless human noise. "Close Proximity" opens with various species of bird perched in the bare branches of a tree, at eye level with the view from an apartment in the backstreets of Assi Ghat. Eagles or vultures hover in the sky above the arid banks of the Ganges as it stretches out in the overexposed heat of the day. "Stand Out in the Crowd" reveals a kaleidoscopic vision of a street procession through the wire mesh of an apartment window. People are reduced to digital blocks of chromatic colour as if part of an ancient computer game. Hahn pulls focus to reveal a street paved with stone, refuse strewn in the gutters and a steady procession of humanity passing by, saris a riot of colour, noise and life—blue, purple, berry, saffron—children in arms and men in monochrome, underscored by a soundtrack of raucous birds, distant gongs and percussions, loops of sound and electronic washes, whooshes and whirls. This is not a Western tourist's vision of an ancient sacred city, it is a machine-extended vision, and is how Hahn takes the everyday and shifts it into a futuristic register.

In "Morse Rigveda X, 158, 4-5" a light from a lamp in a back street Varanasi garage has its filaments reduced to black and white by using filters applied in editing software, and is accompanied by the sound of Morse code. This combination of graphic effects and sound shifts the aesthetic perception of the source image from representation to abstract digital surface. This vignette communicates a strange assemblage of the multiple temporalities present in each instant, and is accompanied by a poetic text:

> Long and short intervals of a flickering lamp in a Varanasi garage, reciting in Morse forward and backward the Rigveda X, 158, 4-5: "Give sight onto the eye, give thou our bodies sight that they may see: May we survey, discern this world. Thus, Surya, may we look on thee, on thee most lovely to behold." (Hahn, "Morse Rigveda X, 158, 4-5", 2012f)

Here poem, sound and source footage are abstracted through editing and effects to join and connect the present in its state of urban decay with the divine, as parts of the text that is "spelt" in Morse Code is drawn from a verse of the ancient Hindu religious and literary classic, the Rigveda.

The earliest remains of miniatures in art in India date from 993 BCE and were essentially Buddhist paintings that had "descended from the walls to the palm-leaf manuscripts" (Chaitanya 1994, 97), and, centuries later, onto books and albums. Indian miniatures were very small-scale paintings that reflected the spiritual practices of the Jains, Hindus, and Buddhists. They depicted divinities and the life of the Buddha and, in later periods, during the Mughal Empire, began to include the representation of secular activities (Brown 1918, 8). These Mughal miniatures included portraits and scenes that detailed hunting, battles, historical episodes, the intricacies of palace life, zoology, botany and, occasionally, religious incidents (Brown 1918, 71). Miniatures are an individual rather than communal art (Brown 1918) and were used as private intimate documents carried in books by nomadic people from one place to another. As portable forms of art they developed cross-cultural elements and contain

Indo–Persian and Chinese influences, as well as local variations transformed by centuries of invasion, cultural exchange and the crossing of borders. Hahn's vignettes in *Indian Records* reprise these qualities of the miniature as a record of everyday moments captured in electro-acoustic form through a mobile camera and editing.

To enlarge, to magnify, to pay attention and to look closely—these are actions described by Gaston Bachelard as the necessary attributes and actions required to gain entry into the world of the miniature. Bachelard writes of how "[t]he details of a thing can be a sign of a new world" (155), and it is the magnifying glass that he uses to take us into a detail. Similarly, in *Indian Records*, it is often through details that we enter the world of the miniature. In Hahn's vignettes this is achieved via the use of a zoom or telephoto lens, or the use of what could be thought of as "a sound miniature" (Bachelard, 166). Each serves to focus our attention upon a detail magnified as already sufficient in itself. Here, objects and sounds can act as switches or passages between worlds, and Hahn's use of the close-up enables passage from one world to another, where *things* become optical connectors, micro-aesthetic triggers that take us between one state and another. This might be the rippling geographies of silk in "Silk Seduction," the rhythmic, delicate balletic motion of a pair of hands ironing fabric in "Iron Man," or the extreme close-up of a bike rider's orange shirt in "Tectonic Shifts."

Hahn creates micro-worlds that provide momentary refuge from the world itself, but they are also a means to look at the world as a transitory state, giving us the chance to rethink our relationship to it.

Return to New Delhi

17–31 December 2012
On Hahn's return to New Delhi we encounter, in "On Off Gate—Very Analog," an ant's-eye view of a dribbling, rusted pipe in the Lodhi Gardens, an archaeological site of fifteenth-century mosques and tombs. In a reflexive twist, the cameraperson's hand enters frame to use a tiny shifting spanner to turn off the gate. This fleeting presence of the filmmaker lets the work perform and document a moment of encounter and participation with the objects that litter the landscape. Each of the small works in this second New Delhi series are marked by almost whimsical contradiction as they record industrial systems in decline and the tenacity

of people in their ongoing struggle for existence amongst this decay. In "Sketch 1" and "Sketch 2" Hahn records the shadow of a rickshaw driver as he passes along the street, and in the final three vignettes from the series Hahn confronts us with images of a shadow world, humans fused with the detritus of city streets near the Central Market at Feroze Gandhi Marg. These are human and inhuman images as solarised shadows are rendered in a world of noise and electronic beeps. These images, chillingly, conjure references to the solarised shadows of people imprinted on the walls of Hiroshima, and are a stark and prophetic image of a human future as a transient impression upon a littered earth. These final vignettes too, connect with the final images of Chris Marker's *Sunless* (1983) as Marker's journey passes into the "zone" where images are stripped of subjectivity and documentary representation and reduced to a sensory sign "affected by the moss of Time, freed of the lie that had prolonged the existence of those moments swallowed by the Spiral" (Marker 1984, 40). Hahn's work too moves past motifs of memory and representation, piercing what Marker has described as the "poignancy of things" (40) by showing the endless struggle of people in an increasingly mechanised world. In "Rickshaw/loop," for example, the final vignette recorded on the last day of his residency, Hahn wields a camera from the back of a rickshaw, holding it at zoom's length as it peers past the driver's zippered grey serge jacket on Mahatma Gandhi Road, head wrapped in a scarf to protect him from heat or cold. A soundtrack of pure tones, electronic beeps and scrapings reminiscent of a science fiction score deepen the anonymity of the driver, a moving monolith, poignant, a relentlessly pedalling wrapped figure of the past, pushing through the inertia of the present, into a future space and time.

Reflexive Mapping: Miniaturising the New World

Alexander Hahn connects with and experiences urban spaces through a complex first-person encounter, and captures what is alien or strange, as he travels into the new and unfamiliar. Hahn's "media art trails" in *Bharat|India* and *Indian Records* provide a reflexive map of his own processes of perception and encounter with the extraordinary scale of the Indian subcontinent, in miniature. Here Hahn uses his camera as part of an epistolary method, as a means of note taking and jotting down thoughts, sketching to catch the evanescent, mapping the process of sense-making and encounter. Across his three-month residency in India, Hahn posts moments captured by fixed, concealed, moving, and handheld cameras. Hahn's small moments draw attention to the transitory nature of existence and the scale and impact of urban transformations in contemporary northern India through a multitude of micro-observations. His work uses the micro-compositional form of the miniature, as well as micro-aesthetic practices that reprise elements of experimental film, sound, documentary, and art. Hahn engages with peripatetic and aleatory methods that are common to the essay film; however, rather than literary genealogies, Hahn's serialised "video vignettes" are closer to the preparatory practices of jotting and note keeping found in the field journal, travel diary, or sketch pad. By drawing and composing with video, music and sounds, *Bharat|India* and *Indian Records* participates in genealogies and processes that underpin the arts, literature and sciences. These forms and traditions in their turn are part of a larger process of reconnecting and linking film, video, music and social media as thinking systems to an archaeology of mind—a topology—noticing a changing anthropogenic urban nature.

The use of the small and serialised video art form in *Indian Records* provides insight into the altered experience of the senses when confronted with vast countries and cultures. Hahn presents a digital documentary trail of north-west India, capturing a converged perception between humans, diverse cultures, and religions, coexisting in densely populated urban spaces in a state of disintegration and renewal. The quotidian in Hahn's India is observed as being in a state of accelerated urban change. Hahn captures the increasing technologisation of the senses, particularly through his multiple cameras, human, and non-human viewpoints, to reveal where the cinematic and cinematographic converge through travel and transportation. This is often ironically underscored in Hahn's miniatures in *Indian Records,* as he includes glimpses of himself throughout the series, reaching for a concealed camera after it has been dropped, fallen, or been kicked on the street.

Sometimes the viewer can see Hahn's shadow, or a wry smile, a self that exists at the intersection of diverse cultural spaces. For example, in the vignette "Sidhpur Impression" the soundtrack highlights the rumble of a toilet's plumbing system as it shunts water into the cistern. Recorded at the Norbulingka Institute, a community organisation developed for the protection and transmission of Tibetan arts and culture located in Dharamsala, the camera captures the play of shadows and light on the tiles of the toilet walls as it zooms out and pans around the room. Hahn completes the take by recording his own image in the bathroom mirror holding his Olympus camera. It is a self-reflexive moment that pays homage to reflexive forms in cinema and art as Hahn exposes the camera recording process as part of a process of infinite regress as the self looks back at the self looking—caught in a spiral of time—and makes a wry comment on the western world's propensity to "document and archive everything" (Hahn, "Sidhpur Impression").

Hahn's journey into the megacity of New Delhi and the ancient city of Varanasi captures urban life at complex intersections, folds and *rapprochements* between a plurality of worlds: the ancient empires of the past, British India, and post-partition India. The continuity of religions and practices from feudal India to the present that intertwine, such as the rickshaw driver, the bureaucracy of museum and sound archives, the iron man, the plastic butterfly clip at Humayun's tomb, and ancient rituals glimpsed through a mobile phone camera. Hahn's video vignettes offer a method of linking and joining disparate spaces and times, perceptions and affects, and provide insights into the urban topologies of the early twenty-first century as "the new nature" where human experience increasingly is tied to urban spaces as prime habitat.

These cities are also thresholds that point to the future, intimated through the composition of images and sound in Hahn's works. Here the new city of the eternal present—composed of concrete, capital, white-goods, electricity, photo-chemicals, and tar—converges with ancient and feudal cultures, diverse religious practices, bureaucratic systems, and accelerated urban change. Hahn's work captures the day-to-day realities of anthropogenic change, where urban spaces and rural imperatives coincide with the breakdown of rivers, countryside, and climate. He realises this accelerated change through a litany of micro moments, showing the fusion and entanglement of the senses that results from the combination of speed and travel, as well as a tenor of the momentary amongst the vastness of space and time, organic and inorganic matter, all in a process of transformation and renewal. In Hahn's work matter and energy are intuited to be in a state of fusion—dust, people, plants, commodities congeal and appear interchangeable, part of an unfolding procession, which Hahn serialises through the construct of the miniature.

Bibliography

Acciavati, Anthony. "The Ganges Water Crisis." *New York Times*, June 17, 2015, Web.

Bachelard, Gaston. *The Poetics of Space*. Boston: Beacon Press, 1994.

Baudelaire, Charles. *The Painter of Modern Life*. Trans. Jonathan Mayne. New York: Da Capo Press, 1964.

Brown, Percy. *The Heritage of India: Indian Painting*. Calcutta: The Association Press, 1918.

Chaitanya, Krishna. *A History of Indian Painting: The Modern Period*. New Delhi: Abhinav Publications, 1994.

Corrigan, Tim. *The Essay Film: From Montaigne to Marker*. New York: Oxford University Press, 2011.

Dhillon, Amrit. "The Ganges: Holy River from Hell." *The Sydney Morning Herald*, August 6, 2014, Web.

Hahn, Alexander (dir.). *Dirt Site*, 1990.

Hahn, Alexander. "Aqueous Transfer Machine." *Bharat|India Travelogue|Video Vignettes*, November 4, 2012a, Web.

Hahn, Alexander. "Beauty of Traffic Jams." *Bharat|India Travelogue|Video Vignettes*, November 4, 2012b, Web.

Hahn, Alexander. "Butterfly Effect." *Bharat|India Travelogue|Video Vignettes*, November 4, 2012c, Web.

Hahn, Alexander. "Fake Rain." *Bharat|India Travelogue|Video Vignettes*, November 4, 2012d, Web.

Hahn, Alexander. "Juice Stand." *Bharat|India Travelogue|Video Vignettes*, October 12, 2012e, Web.

Hahn, Alexander. "Morse Rigveda X, 158, 4-5." *Bharat|India Travelogue|Video Vignettes*, November 15, 2012f, Web.

Hahn, Alexander. "Night Cycle." *Bharat|India Travelogue|Video Vignettes*, November 4, 2012g, Web.

Hahn, Alexander. "On Off Gate–Very Analog." *Bharat|India Travelogue|Video Vignettes*, December 20, 2012h, Web.

Hahn, Alexander. "Rickshaw|Loop." *Bharat|India Travelogue|Video Vignettes*, December 20, 2012i, Web.

Hahn, Alexander. "Shadow in Motion Sketch 1." *Bharat|India Travelogue|Video Vignettes*, December 30, 2012j, Web.

Hahn, Alexander. "Shadow in Motion Sketch 2." *Bharat|India Travelogue|Video Vignettes*, December 25, 2012k, Web.

Hahn, Alexander. "Sidhpur Impression." *Bharat|India Travelogue|Video Vignettes*, December 20, 2012l, Web.

Hahn, Alexander. "Sitting in Close Proximity." *Bharat|India Travelogue|Video Vignettes*, November 4, 2012m, Web.

Hahn, Alexander. "Spectral Figures." *Bharat|India Travelogue|Video Vignettes*, September 29, 2012n, Web.

Hahn, Alexander. "Stand Out from the Crowd." *Bharat|India Travelogue|Video Vignettes*, November 4, 2012o, Web.

Hahn, Alexander. "Tectonic Shifts." *Bharat|India Travelogue|Video Vignettes*, November 4, 2012p, Web.

Hahn, Alexander. "Trophic Levels in the Food Chain." *Bharat|India Travelogue|Video Vignettes*, November 4, 2012q, Web.

Hahn, Alexander. *Bharat|India Travelogue|Video Vignettes*, November 4, 2012–January 4, 2013a, Web.

Hahn, Alexander (dir.). *Indian Records*, 2013b, Web.

Ivakhiv, Adrian J. *Ecologies of the Moving Image*. Waterloo: Wilfred Laurier University Press, 2013.

Larson, Gerald James. *Classical Samkhya: An Interpretation of Its History and Meaning*. Delhi: Motilal Banarsidass, 2011.

Lyotard, Jean-François. *The Postmodern Condition: A Report on Knowledge*. Trans. Geoff Bennington and Brian Massumi. Minneapolis: University of Minnesota Press, 1984.

Marker, Chris. "Sunless." *Oasis Semiotex(e)* IV.3 (1984): 33–40.

Rizzo, Teresa. "YouTube: The New Cinema of Attractions." *SCAN: Journal of Media Arts Culture* 5.1 (2008), Web.

Saglio-Yatzimirsky, Marie-Caroline, and Frederic Landy. *Megacity Slums: Social Exclusion, Space and Urban Policies in Brazil and India*. Singapore: World Scientific Publishing Company, 2013.

Serres, Michel *with* Bruno Latour. *Conversations on Science, Culture, and Time*. Trans. Roxanne Lapidus. Ann Arbor: University of Michigan Press, 1995.

Singh, Rana P.B. "Varanasi, India's Cultural Heritage City: Contestation, Conservation & Planning," *Heritagescapes and Cultural Landscapes*. Ed. Rana P.B. Singh. New Delhi: Shubhi Publications, 2011. 205–254.

Twain, Mark. *Following the Equator: A Journey Around the World*. Hartford: The American Publishing Company, 1897.

Virilio, Paul. *War and Cinema: The Logistics of Perception*. Trans. Patrick Camiller. London: Verso, 1989.

Virilio, Paul. *Negative Horizon: An Essay in Dromoscopy*. Trans. Michael Degener. London: Continuum, 2008.

24Frames 24Hours: An Emerging Form of Workshop-Generated Documentary

Max Schleser

Abstract This chapter outlines the framework of workshop-facilitated documentary as a collaborative method for developing digital literacy, self-representation of local communities, and the creation of "sociability" in documentaries about place. By means of utilising mobile, smartphone and pocket camera filmmaking techniques, these workshops question notions of authorship and extend our understanding of creativity.

Keywords mobile, smartphone and pocket filmmaking • collaboration • digital creativity • digtal literacy • mobile and smartphone documentary

Introduction

Collaborative Mobile-Mentaries Enabling Creative Transformation

The global city film *24Frames 24Hours* is part of a practice-led research project investigating the opportunities for participation and the development of cultural competencies and new media literacies (Jenkins et al. 2009)

M. Schleser (✉)
Swinburne University of Technology, Melbourne, Australia

A. Miles (ed.), *Digital Media and Documentary*,
https://doi.org/10.1007/978-3-319-68643-1_7

that mobile media enables. It is an experiment in cinematic communication exploring how participants in various countries, including Germany, France, United Kingdom, United States, New Zealand, Australia, and Malaysia, can explore their world through the lens of their mobile devices. Since 2013, online and face-to-face workshops have taken place in Kuala Lumpur, London, Strasburg, Paderborn, Auckland, Wellington, and West Long Branch. These mobile filmmaking workshops are designed to explore the creative potential of mobile media in the context of a local community's ability to reflect upon and define itself, and to then share this media with other local communities internationally.

This chapter explores what I describe as the mobile-mentary (mobile documentary) as a cultural practice. Furthermore, this chapter analyses the video portraits created in these mobile filmmaking workshops in relation to the "participatory turn" in media culture that includes collaboration, co-creation, and crowdsourcing that media scholars such as Jenkins (Jenkins et al. 2009) have documented in the context of media education and digital literacy. This chapter considers the contemporary mediascape as an ecosystem that has seen the emergence of new aesthetic forms and formats, such as iPhoneography and mobile-mentary filmmaking, alongside existing media forms and institutions. *24Frames 24Hours* describes a shift from a discussion about the "digital divide" toward one about smartphones that not only afford access to filmmaking technology in "global villages," but also provide prospects for twenty-first-century citizens to develop innovative and imaginative cultural competencies (Katz et al. 2011; Lally et al. 2011; Shirky 2010). Mobile media (Goggin 2012; Hjorth et al. 2012), creativity, and imaginative digital storytelling are explored in this practice-led research as a means to engage audiences, especially young audiences, in making sense of their place in the world. The filmmaking approach used references and further expands Dziga Vertov's concepts into the digital domain (Hicks 2007; MacKay 2012; Roberts 2000; Vickers 2013). Vertov formulated ideas in a filmmaking manifesto that provides a prototype for a contemporary collaborative mobile-mentary, "Freed from the rule of sixteen-seventeen frames per second, free of the limits of time and space, I put together any given points in the universe, no matter where I've recorded them. My path leads to the creation of a fresh perception of the world. I decipher a new way a world unknown to you" (Vertov 1984, 17–18). The participatory nature of *24 Frames 24 Hours* reflects what David Abelevich Kaufman outlines as "experimentation is also to be regarded as a kind of ferment that involves interested colleagues in intensive cooperation—a method that is tried and true (Vertov 1984, 21). While Vertov's montage filmmaking method "should also be regarded as an educational, model workshop through which Young Pioneer and Komsomol film groups will be drawn into production work.... They will be the author-creators of all subsequent film-objects" (Hicks 2007, 20).

The ability to record high-quality audio-visual media and GPS metadata with current mobile devices allows for the possibility to engage with local communities to explore their environment and location. My research is specifically about the social intervention required to leverage the potential of mobile media and creativity into tangible results for community groups. In an increasingly digital and global sphere, documentary and mobile-mentary texts can interact with communities through the networked systems and user-based architectures that have become part of the twenty-first-century storytelling toolkit. These new systems let us ask questions of the new forms emerging in the context of documentary as a cultural discourse, in particular how we might rethink the idea of the documentary form. *24Frames 24Hours* uses mobile-mentary portraits about places and people that are then placed through "geolocative montage" into a dynamic interface. The *24Frames 24Hours* interface then enables users to construct narratives around their video, based upon defined parameters of time and space.

Mobile Filmmaking Workshops

Through an initial research and experimentation phase a model for teaching basic mobile filmmaking was developed. This provided the basis to explore creativity as a form of community engagement. The community workshops utilised an iterative design approach and this allowed the research to examine the impact of wireless, mobile, and ubiquitous computing in representations of place, and how digital creativity could be used to engage young filmmakers within participatory culture. Elsewhere I have argued for a differentiation between collaborative and co-creation in documentary theory and practice (Schleser 2011), and developed the participatory approach for *24Frames 24Hours* in response to this. The first workshop in 2011 led to the development of a participatory framework for further workshops and initiated the themes that were subsequently explored. Workshop participants are first inspired by a screening of mobile films already published on the *24Frames 24Hours* platform. This is followed by a short ideation session that engages with mobile aesthetics and the characteristics of mobile video. This session is used to compile a "shopping list" of shots to collect on location, and participants go through a series of experiments in which they learn about framing, composition, and apps for mobile filming. Once completed, participants are ready to head out on location. When they return from the field they participate in an editing workshop. The structure of the editing workshop is quite flexible and responds to any logistical requirements that may have arisen. Participants then edit a video portrait about the place or person of their choice, which is more or less an exercise in digital storytelling. The workshops empower participants to engage in conversations about the subjects that are relevant to them, and to be introduced to peers who share similar ideas and interests. Their completed work is then published via the *24Frames 24Hours* platform.

As a filmmaker working with mobile devices, smartphones, and pocket cameras, I have found it unnecessary to separate video making into the traditional pre and postproduction phases. This dividing of production is an industrial, Fordist model, which emphasises the streamlining and optimisation of work rather than craft. In the workshops I have found that the craft of making takes place during the course of shooting and editing. Hence, the workshop-generated videos emphasise the experience of their makers more than narrative cohesion or representational veracity. This is perhaps not surprising as cameras are mobile and able to freely move around space and so are always close to the action. The small cameras used, and their limitations, need to be understood as a creative obstruction rather than a limitation. Hence, a consideration of mobile video's aesthetics, and the specificity of mobile media, is valid for these projects and, in the context of first-person documentary, mobile media has the potential to capture experiences in a more personal and intimate manner than when using larger and more "professional" recording equipment such as a DSLR or Red HD camera. In other words, mobile filmmaking is not a cinema defined by pristine high-definition quality but by its spontaneity and the free flow of its moving images. Editing then becomes a key technique for mobile filmmaking, as it is in editing that conceptual decision-making processes occur that include critical self-reflection, and it is in editing that one is confronted with the reflective moment where one can understand and make sense of the recorded experience. This repeats Astruc's original vision of the camera pen, for now it allows everyone with a smartphone to express themselves using video (Astruc 1948, in Corrigan 1999, 158), and young people's use of mobile video provides a means to engage with the world that does not rely on writing, and provides other opportunities for communities to share knowledge through these workshop generated videos. Storytelling about places and communities can then be supported by mobile media as we develop new audio-visual literacies.

Workshop-Generated Videos

24Frames 24Hours explores distributed production through these workshops and distributed authorship through the site's interface. Workshop participants have the opportunity to discuss their ideas and receive support with filming and editing on their smartphones. On occasions, workshops connected groups of young filmmakers in different international locations using Skype and Google Hangouts.

Revisiting Vertov

Dziga Vertov's idea of producing mobile films with Soviet citizens on agitprop trains, and later his *Cine-Pravda* newsreels (Vertov 1984), provided conceptual ideas for workshop generated videos. As Suderburg reminds us, "Kinoks would make the film-thing together and, in making it together, fabricate a moving image—a living evolutionary process built on an armature, a series of modular 'blocks' that ultimately could be reused indefinitely without removing them from either their efficacy or their morphing truths" (2012, 96). This collective approach is a framework that can be used for mobile filmmaking (Schleser 2010; Berry et al. 2014), and the model of direct creative engagement between participants and filmmaking in the workshops leads to active participation in making sense of one's everyday environment. Video apps for aggregation, streaming, shooting, and editing, and platforms like Vimeo and YouTube, combined with cloud computing and broadband, provide an architecture for the creative industries and citizens to work with online video, and so the ability for individuals to use these to engage with the world become important to documentary.

Similarly, mobile documentary filmmaking provides an alternative to existing industry conventions and practices, it explores moving image practice free from format constraints, and mobile aesthetics are developed in a collaborative approach during workshops. This can be seen as an intervention into the industry-dominated discourses of professional media practice.

Interactive Documentary

Julia Scott-Stevenson, in her analysis of online documentaries made with community organisations notes, new forms of collaboration encourage a transformation in audience engagement and participation:

> While there is a long history of activist and social documentary that has worked to achieve this engagement and action, a reframing in the online world allows this interaction to take new forms, including within the very documentary itself. (Scott-Stevenson 2011, 186)

Similarly, Aston and Gaudenzi (2012) believe that "i-docs offer a tool as much for the co-creation of reality as for its representation" (128), and that "collaborative i-docs can fundamentally question the role we want to have in society to give us active choices that can re-define who we want to be" (135). I want to reinforce the significance of this statement and add that for workshop-generated videos the notion of process is pivotal. Through a self-reflexive approach, combined with an understanding of montage and editing in documentary, which in *24 Frames 24 Hours* relates to the filmic decision making process, participants engage in moments of transformation. Hence, the workshop model proposes a documentary production approach as a process comparable to a conversation or dialogue between place and participants. This can be linked to the precedents Aston and Gaudenzi outline in the participatory mode of interactive documentary where they outline the involvement of the user during the production process through the use of online editing (see *RiP: A Remix Manifesto*, Gaylor 2004–2009), or shooting in the streets (*18 Days in Egypt*, Mehta and Elayat, 2011). As a form of participatory engagement, workshop-generated content uses editing to engage in conceptual developments with an emphasis on reflexivity and representation. As a framework workshop-generated videos relate to the position that Aston and Gaudenzi's ascribe to digital media:

> human need to try to make sense of the world around us, using whatever tools are to hand, and in the role of narrative and storytelling in that process. In accepting the idea that, in our contemporary times, digital media plays an important part in shaping culture, and in influencing the ways in which we relate to the world, our aim was to explore how interactive technologies might offer new ways to help us both to understand the world and to shape it. (Aston and Gaudenzi 2012, 129)

24Frames 24Hours provides a contribution to the field of interactive documentary through the pedagogy of the workshops, directing attention to place through narrative and editing in mobile filmmaking.

As media making and consumption moves from applications and channels to platforms, the broader media environment moves toward what Manovich describes as "media mobility" (Manovich 2008, 203), and what Jenkins labels as "spreadable media" (Jenkins et al. 2009). While our media environment is in this transitory phase one can notice mainstream media embracing these changes and acknowledging the potential of networked practices in user-generated content. However, a key difference between user-generated content and workshop-generated videos is that participants in the workshops are explicitly engaged in a creative process. The vernacular creative artefacts that the workshops create should then not be examined as traditional or mainstream media texts as they have their own qualities as mobile-mentaries (Schleser 2009, 2012a), and the face-to-face contact in the workshops allows the participant's contribution to be understood as part of a process to create new forms and formats for the representation of identity and place. Workshop-generated video content can be defined as a cultural discourse that reshapes recent hybrid interactive documentaries from within.

Video Platform for Creating Connections

As a public intervention *24Frames 24Hours* engages citizen users to help them explore mobile devices and smartphones as creative tools, while teaching new media literacies through mobile filmmaking workshops. Participants use their mobile phones to produce two-minute videos about their communities. These mobile filmmaking workshops have been conducted at film festivals, universities, museums, and public institutions, and participants create video portraits about a place and a person and upload these to YouTube. The uploaded workshop videos are then added to the *24 Hours 24 Frames* site using an interface developed by Tim Turnidge, with the aim of creating a forum for mobile filmmakers.

Each video created in the workshops has metadata associated with it. This metadata is accessed through YouTube's Application Programming Interface (API) and typically contains information such as the author of the video, the GPS coordinates of its location, and what time of day it was shot. Custom metadata that is generated in collaboration with the

24Frames 24Hours documentary is also created. The geolocative metadata is the primary interface used to browse the videos and so the locative nature of mobile video is emphasised, identifying each video with a location and empowering its maker to make a statement about a place. *24Frames 24Hours* becomes then a mobile–mentary as it dynamically generates a "documentary" through the parameters that users select. While viewing *24Frames 24Hours*, a user can interact via the interface to direct their experience of the documentary by specifying the videos they want to see based on location, time or theme. The interface encourages users to engage with the project as well as mobile and smartphone filmmaking through generating their own remix of the documentary material and by contributing their own videos. In addition, when working with citizen users and community groups, a flexible approach to standards and formats is required, due to the variety of phone cameras and devices that participants use. The creation of a custom web video database with associated metadata in *24 Frames 24 Hours* can accommodate this variety and enable exploration of this database narrative through the "algorithmic editing" that the database allows.

24Frames 24Hours uses the mobile phone as a tool for creative storytelling to enable ordinary citizens who are not filmmakers to become filmmakers. By using the geolocative metadata recorded by mobile media, connections between workshop participants are facilitated through social networks. The different aspect ratios used are a counterpoint to the standards found in mainstream broadcast media, and when combined with the spatial montage of the project's interface, serendipitous juxtapositions and connections can be made between videos. The APIs provided by platforms such as YouTube and Vimeo offer exciting possibilities for exploring and making database cinema using metadata and algorithmic editing. *24 Frames 24 Hours* enables the collaborative generation of video content and mobile-mentaries using the established infrastructure of these video platforms.

Conclusion: Towards Workshop Generated Video

This chapter argues that workshop-generated video is an emerging documentary form that creates a cultural discourse about place and community identity. These workshops utilise mobile filmmaking in the context of existing documentary traditions and illustrate how contemporary crowdsourcing strategies of making media can question notions of authorship and extend our understanding of creativity. Collaborative mobile filmmaking shifts from looking at film as an end product towards examining the processes of its making and sharing. Editing becomes a negotiation and open dialogue with the participants, rather than a linear construction. *24Frames 24Hours* uses its workshop model as a reflexive process that allows participants to engage in a subject of their choice that is relevant to them. Through this creative involvement collaborative mobile filmmaking supports and enables a sense of presence and sociability through the self-representation of local communities while developing digital literacy skills.

Bibliography

Aston, Judith, and Sandra Gaudenzi. "Interactive Documentary: Setting the Field." *Studies in Documentary Film* 6.2 (2012): 125–139.

Berry, Marsha, and Max Schleser, eds. *Mobile Media Making in an Age of Smartphones*. London: Palgrave Macmillan, 2014.

Corrigan, Timothy. *Film and Literature: An Introduction and Reader*. Upper Saddle River, NJ: Prentice Hall, 1999.

Gaylor, Brett (dir.). *RiP: A Remix Manifesto*, Gaylor. National Film Board of Canada and EyeSteelFilm, Canada, 2004–2009.

Goggin, Gerard. *New Technologies and the Media*. London: Palgrave Macmillan, 2012.

Hicks, Jeremy. *Dziga Vertov: Defining Documentary Film*. London: I.B. Tauris, 2007.

Hjorth, Larrisa, Jean E. Burgess, and Ingrid Richardson. *Studying Mobile Media: Cultural Technologies, Mobile Communication, and the iPhone*. London: Routledge, 2012.

Jenkins, Henry, et al. *Confronting the Challenges of Participatory Culture: Media Education for the 21st Century*. The John D. and Catherine T. MacArthur Foundation Reports on Digital Media and Learning. Cambridge: The MIT Press, 2009.

Katz, James E., Wayne LaBar, and Ellen Lynch. *Creativity and Technology: Social Media, Mobiles and Museums*. New York City: MuseumsEtc, 2011.

Lally, Elaine, Ien Ang, and Kay Anderson. *The Art of Engagement: Culture, Collaboration, Innovation*. Perth: UWA Publishing, 2011.

MacKay, John. "Vertov and the Line: Art, Socialization, Collaboration." *Film, Art, New Media: Museums Without Walls?* Ed. Angela Dalle Vacche. Basingstoke: Palgrave Macmillan, 2012. 81–98.

Manovich, Lev. *Software Takes Command*, 2008, Web.

Mehta, Jigar, and Yasmin Elayat. *18 Days in Egypt*, 2011-ongoing, http://beta.18daysinegypt.com/.

Roberts, Graham. *The Man with the Movie Camera. (KINOFiles Film Companion)*. London: I.B. Tauris, 2000.
Schleser, Max, Camille Baker, and Kasia Molga. “Aesthetics of Mobile Media Art.” *Journal of Media Practice* 10.2 and 3 (2009): 101–122.
Schleser, Max. “Mobile Creativity.” *Mobile Learning: Pilot Projects and Initiatives*. Ed. Guy Retta. Santa Rosa: Informing Science Press, 2010. 201–213.
Schleser, Max. “Mobile-Mentary (Mobile Documentary) 2.0: The Distinction Between Collaborative and Co-creation in Documentary Theory and Practice” *Expanding Documentary 2011: Conference Proceedings* 1.2 (2011): 172–180.
Schleser, Max. “Collaborative Mobile Phone Filmmaking.” *The Handbook of Participatory Video*. Ed. E.-J. Milne, Claudia Mitchell and Naydene de Lange. Blue Ridge Summit, PA: AltaMira Press/Rowman, 2012a. 397–410.
Schleser, Max. *24Frames 24Hours*, 2012b-ongoing, Web.
Scott-Stevenson, Julia. “The Interactive Documentary in a Cross-platform, Community Context.” *Expanding Documentary 2011: Conference Proceedings* 1.2 (2011): 181–188.
Shirky, Clay. *Cognitive Surplus: Creativity and Generosity in a Connected Age*. London: Penguin Books, 2010.
Suderburg, Erika. “Database, Anarchéologie, the Commons, Kino-Eye, and Mash: How Bard, Kaufman, Svilova, and Vertov Continue the Revolution.” *Resolutions 3 – Global Networks of Video*. Ed. Ming-Yeun S. Ma and Erika Suderburg. Minneapolis: University of Minnesota Press, 2012. 92–104.
Vertov, Dziga (dir.). *The Man with a Movie Camera*, 1927.
Vertov, Dziga. *Kino-Eye: The Writings of Dziga Vertov*. Ed. Annette Michelson, Trans. Kevin O’Brien. Berkeley: University of California Press, 1984.
Vickers, Richard. “Mobile Media, Participation Culture and the Digital Vernacular: 24-Hours in and the Democratization of Documentary.” *MINA – Mobile Innovation Network Aotearoa. Special Issue of Ubiquity: The Journal of Pervasive Media* 2.1–2 (2013): 132–145.

Index

A

Actor-network theory, 70
Affect
  affection, 77
  affective, 31, 32, 34, 75–81, 87
Affordance, 3, 6–8, 31, 36, 38, 49–54, 57, 58, 60, 62, 73
Algorithm, 80
  algorithmic, 76, 108
Application Programming Interface (API), 71, 107, 108
Apps, 4, 70–76, 80, 104, 105
Astruc, Alexander, 104

B

Bachelard, Gaston, 94
Bergson, Henry, 69, 75, 76, 78

C

Content Management System (CMS), 56–57

D

Debord, Guy, 91
Deleuze, Gilles, 2, 69, 75–78
Design methods
  design, 9, 17, 19, 22, 33, 42, 44, 49–54, 57, 58, 62–65, 103
  design methodology, 49–51, 53, 54, 62–64
Diary, 71–73, 85, 87, 96

E

Ephemeral media
  ephemeral form, 34
  ephemerality, 36
  ephemeral practice, 34
  transient media, 95
  transient practice, 95
  transitory, 5, 107
Epistolary form, 83–97
Essay, 6, 13, 14, 17, 19–22, 25–26, 70, 79, 96
  essayist, 3, 14, 18–20, 22, 26, 80

A. Miles (ed.), *Digital Media and Documentary*,
https://doi.org/10.1007/978-3-319-68643-1

Essay film, 14, 19–22, 25–26, 96
  essay, 6, 13, 14, 17, 19–22, 25–26, 70, 79, 96
Everyday media, 71, 72
Everyday media making
  everyday practice, 70, 71
  everyday spaces, 35

F

Form
  diary, 73, 83, 85
  epistolary, 83–97
  essay, 25, 26
  list, 17, 18, 20, 25, 26
  micro, 96
  micro-aesthetic, 96
  miniature, 85, 86
  poetic, 32, 34, 86
  serialepistolary, 96
  short-form, 85, 86
  small, 87, 96

G

Generative, 7–9, 59, 72, 81
Geolocation, 7
  geolocative, 103, 108
GPS, 31, 73, 75, 76, 103, 107
Granular, 81
  granularity, 7, 8, 24–26, 52, 58, 59, 61
Guattari, Félix, 2

H

Hahn, Alexander, 9, 83–97

I

Industry conventions
  legacy media, 10
  legacy practice, 105
Industry practices, 51, 105
Instruction based art, 39, 45
Interaction, 14, 19, 22, 30, 32, 35, 39, 44, 52, 56–58, 63–65, 78, 106
Interactive, 2–11, 13–27, 34, 43, 44, 49–65, 69, 70, 72, 75–81, 106–107
Interface, 14, 15, 17, 19, 21–23, 26, 33, 42, 43, 50, 52, 58, 60, 64, 71, 78, 103, 105, 107, 108

K

Korsakow software, 14, 16, 18, 19, 21, 23, 26, 51, 52, 55–57, 60

L

Latour, Bruno, 70, 87
Legacy media, 5, 71
Legacy practices, 4, 71
Life journaling, 74
Listing
  list making, 9, 18, 19, 21, 22, 25
  lists, 9, 10, 14, 17–21, 25, 26
Locative media
  location based media, 10
  location based narrative, 44
  location based story, 43
  location specific, 31, 32, 36, 43
  site specific, 45

M

Machine
  machine perspective, 90
  media machine, 70–76, 79–81
Manovich, Lev, 15, 25, 52, 56, 58, 60, 107
Marker, Chris, 10, 14, 19, 21, 95

Massey, Doreen, 38
Media Art Trail, 84–86, 95
Metadata, 52, 103, 107, 108
Micro, serial, 96, 97
Miniature, 83–97
Mobile filmmaking, 102–105, 107–109
Mobile media, 36, 70, 75, 102–105, 108
Mobile video, 104, 105, 108

N
Narrative, 5, 9, 10, 14, 20, 24–26, 36, 38, 41, 43, 44, 50, 53, 57, 61, 62, 64, 103, 104, 106–108
Non-narrative, 25, 53
  list eschews narrative, 20
Noticing, 5, 9, 11, 13–27, 72, 76–80, 86, 90, 96

P
Participatory media
  community participation, 106–109
  community workshop, 103
  participant contributions, 36
  participation, 3, 7, 30, 35, 39, 42, 94, 101, 105, 106
  participatory framework, 103
Places, 3, 6, 10, 22, 29–45, 74, 81, 86–88, 90, 92, 93, 102–108
Platform, 7, 31, 33, 45, 50, 54–57, 75, 76, 80, 81, 103–105, 107–108
Poetic form
  poetics, 20, 21, 32–34, 40, 41, 45, 79–81, 85–87, 89, 90, 93
  practice, 34
Polyvocal, 38
  polyvocalities, 38–40
Practice, 1–7, 10, 11, 13–27, 30–32, 34–43, 45, 49–65, 70–73, 76, 80, 81, 84, 85, 87, 93, 96, 97, 101–103, 105, 107
Practice based research
  creative arts research, 107
  creative research, 4
  practice and research, 4, 6, 50, 51, 62
  practice led research, 50, 101, 102
  practitioner, 1, 56, 62
  practitioner scholar, 2
Procedural, 7–9, 32, 40, 44, 45, 59, 76, 81

R
Relationality
  pattern, 9, 14, 80, 81
  patterns formed, 16
  patterns of relation, 14, 80
  relational, 10, 36–40, 75, 78, 79
  relations, 6, 8–10, 14, 19, 21–26, 36, 40, 45, 50–54, 57–63, 70, 78–81, 85, 102
  relations between, 8, 10, 14, 21–24, 52, 53, 58, 59, 61
  relationship between, 15, 21, 22, 25
Remix, 52, 59, 62, 108

S
Scale, 1, 4, 5, 7–11, 59, 70, 84, 86, 95, 96
Serial form, 96
  serialised, 75, 87, 96, 97
Serres, Michel, 84, 87
Sketch, 2, 10, 63, 95, 96
Smartphone
  mobile device, 35, 42, 76, 102–104, 107
  mobile phone, 31, 73, 74, 76, 97, 107, 108

Spatial montage, 52, 60, 108
Story, 9, 25, 43, 44, 51, 58, 81
Storytelling, 102–106, 108

U
User-generated, 30, 107

V
Vernacular media, 72
  vernacular creative artefacts, 107
Vertov, Dziga, 102, 103, 105
Virilio, Paul, 88, 91

The manufacturer's authorised representative in the EU is Springer Nature Customer Service Centre GmbH, Europaplatz 3, 69115 Heidelberg, Germany. If you have any concerns regarding our products, please contact ProductSafety@springernature.com

Printed and bound by CPI Group (UK) Ltd, Croydon, CR0 4YY
25/09/2026
02222890-0010